THE URGENCY OF CHANGE

Christmas '79

To Lisa,

    Here's a little book to help dust away the cobwebs; to quench your thirst with its clean liquid; and to extend courage to the next horizon.

          With love,

           John

THE URGENCY OF CHANGE

by

J. KRISHNAMURTI

Edited by Mary Lutyens

PERENNIAL LIBRARY
Harper & Row, Publishers
New York, Hagerstown, San Francisco, London

CONTENTS

AWARENESS

Questioner: I should like to know what you mean by awareness because you have often said that awareness is really what your teaching is about. I've tried to understand it by listening to your talks and reading your books, but I don't seem to get very far. I know it is not a practice, and I understand why you so emphatically repudiate any kind of practice, drill, system, discipline or routine. I see the importance of that, for otherwise it becomes mechanical, and at the end of it the mind has become dull and stupid. I should like, if I may, to explore with you to the very end this question of what it means to be aware. You seem to give some extra, deeper meaning to this word, and yet it seems to me that we *are* aware of what's going on all the time. When I'm angry I know it, when I'm sad I know it and when I'm happy I know it.

Krishnamurti: I wonder if we really are aware of anger, sadness, happiness? Or are we aware of these things only when they are all over? Let us begin as though we know nothing about it at all and start from scratch. Let us not make any assertions, dogmatic or subtle, but let us explore this question which, if one really went into it very deeply, would reveal an extraordinary state that the mind has probably never touched, a dimension not touched by superficial awareness. Let us start from the superficial and work through.

We see with our eyes, we perceive with our senses the things about us—the colour of the flower, the humming bird over the flower, the light of this Californian sun, the thousand sounds of

1

different qualities and subtleties, the depth and the height, the shadow of the tree and the tree itself. We feel in the same way our own bodies, which are the instruments of these different kinds of superficial, sensory perceptions. If these perceptions remained at the superficial level there would be no confusion at all. That flower, that pansy, that rose, are there, and that's all there is to it. There is no preference, no comparison, no like and dislike, only the thing before us without any psychological involvement. Is all this superficial sensory perception or awareness quite clear? It can be expanded to the stars, to the depth of the seas, and to the ultimate frontiers of scientific observation, using all the instruments of modern technology.

Questioner: Yes, I think I understand that.

Krishnamurti: So you see that the rose and all the universe and the people in it, your own wife if you have one, the stars, the seas, the mountains, the microbes, the atoms, the neutrons, this room, the door, really are there. Now, the next step: what you think about these things, or what you feel about them, is your psychological response to them. And this we call thought or emotion. So the superficial awareness is a very simple matter: the door is there. But the description of the door is not the door, and when you get emotionally involved in the description you don't see the door. This description might be a word or a scientific treatise or a strong emotional response; none of these is the door itself. This is very important to understand right from the beginning. If we don't understand this we shall get more and more confused. The description is never the described. Though we are describing something even now, and we have to, the thing we are describing is not our description of it. So please bear this in mind right through our talk. Never confuse the word with the thing it describes. The word is never the real, and we are easily carried away when we come to the next stage of awareness where it becomes personal and we get emotional through the word.

So there is the superficial awareness of the tree, the bird, the door, and there is the response to that, which is thought, feeling, emotion. Now when we become aware of this response, we might call it a second depth of awareness. There is the awareness of the rose, and the awareness of the response to the rose. Often we are unaware of this response to the rose. In reality it is the same awareness which sees the rose and which sees the response. It is one movement and it is wrong to speak of the outer and the inner awareness. When there is a visual awareness of the tree without any psychological involvement there is no division in relationship. But when there is a psychological response to the tree, this response is a conditioned response, it is the response of past memory, past experiences, and this response is a division in relationship. This response is the birth of what we shall call the "me" in relationship and the "non-me". This is how you place yourself in relationship to the world. This is how you create the individual and the community. The world is seen not as it is, but in its various relationships to the "me" of memory. This division is the life and the flourishing of everything we call our psychological being, and from this arises all contradiction and division. Are you very clear that you perceive this? When there is the awareness of the tree there is no evaluation. But when there is a response to the tree, when the tree is judged with like and dislike, then a division takes place in this awareness as the "me" and the "non-me", the "me" who is different from the thing observed. This "me" is the response, in relationship, of past memory, past experiences. Now can there be an awareness, an observation of the tree, without any judgement, and can there be an observation of the response, the reactions, without any judgement? In this way we eradicate the principle of division, the principle of "me" and "non-me", both in looking at the tree and in looking at ourselves.

Questioner: I'm trying to follow you. Let's see if I have got it right. There is an awareness of the tree, that I understand. There is a psychological response to the tree, that I understand also. The psychological response is made up of past memories and past experiences, it is like and dislike, it is the division into the tree and the "me". Yes, I think I understand all that.

Krishnamurti: Is this as clear as the tree itself, or is it simply the clarity of description? Remember, as we have already said, the described is not the description. What have you got, the thing or its description?

Questioner: I think it is the thing.

Krishnamurti: Therefore there is no "me" who is the description in the seeing of this fact. In the seeing of any fact there is no "me". There is either the "me" or the seeing; there can't be both. "Me" is non-seeing. The "me" cannot see, cannot be aware.

Questioner: May I stop here? I think I've got the feeling of it, but I must let it sink in. May I come again tomorrow?

* * *

Questioner: I think I have really understood, non-verbally, what you said yesterday. There is the awareness of the tree, there is the conditioned response to the tree, and this conditioned response is conflict, it is the action of memory and past experiences, it is like and dislike, it is prejudice. I also understand that this response of prejudice is the birth of what we call the "me" or the censor. I see clearly that the "me", the "I", exists in all relationships. Now is there an "I" outside of relationships?

Krishnamurti: We have seen how heavily conditioned our responses are. When you ask if there is a "me" outside of relationship, it becomes a speculative question as long as there is no freedom from these conditioned responses. Do you see that? So our first question is not whether there is a "me" or not outside of conditioned responses, but rather, can the mind, in which is included all our feelings, be free of this conditioning, which is the past? The past is the "me". There is no "me" in the present. As long as the mind is operating in the past there is the "me", and the mind *is* this past, the mind *is* this "me".

You can't say there is the mind and there is the past, and they are two different things. The mind is the past, whether it is the past of a few days ago or of ten thousand years ago. So we are asking: can the mind free itself from yesterday? Now there are several things involved, aren't there? First of all there is a superficial awareness. Then there is the awareness of the conditioned response. Then there is the realisation that the mind is the past, the mind *is* this conditioned response. Then there is the question whether this mind can free itself of the past. And all this is one unitary action of awareness, because in this there are no conclusions. When we say the mind is the past, the realisation is not a verbal conclusion but an actual perception of fact. The French have a word for such a perception of a fact, they call it "constatation". When we ask whether the mind can be free of the past is this question being asked by the censor, the "me", who is that very past?

Questioner: Can the mind be free of the past?

Krishnamurti: Who is putting that question? Is it the entity who is the result of a great many conflicts, memories and experiences—is it he who is asking—or does this question arise of itself, out of the perception of the fact? If it is the observer who is putting the question, then he is trying to escape from the fact of himself, because, he says, I have lived so long in pain, in trouble, in sorrow, I should like to go beyond this constant struggle. If he asks the question from that motive his answer will be a taking refuge in some escape. One either turns away from a fact or one faces it. And the word and the symbol are a turning away from it. In fact, just to ask this question at all is already an act of escape, is it not? Let us be aware whether this question is or is not an act of escape. If it is, it is noise. If there is no observer, then there is silence, a complete negation of the whole past.

Questioner: Here I am lost. How can I wipe away the past in a few seconds?

Krishnamurti: Let us bear in mind that we are discussing awareness. We are talking over together this question of awareness.

There is the tree, and the conditioned response to the tree, which is the "me" in relationship, the "me" who is the very centre of conflict. Now is it this "me" who is asking the question?—this "me" who, as we have said, is the very structure of the past? If the question is not asked from the structure of the past, if the question is not asked by the "me", then there *is* no structure of the past. When the structure is asking the question, it is operating in relationship to the fact of itself, it is frightened of itself and it acts to escape from itself. When this structure does not ask the question, it is not acting in relationship to itself. To recapitulate: there is the tree, there is the word, the response to the tree, which is the censor, or the "me", which comes from the past; and then there is the question: can I escape from all this turmoil and agony? If the "me" is asking this question it is perpetuating itself.

Now, being aware of that, it doesn't ask the question! Being aware, and seeing all the implications of it, the question cannot be asked. It does not ask the question at all because it sees the trap. Now do you see that all this awareness is superficial? It is the same as the awareness which sees the tree.

Questioner: Is there any other kind of awareness? Is there any other dimension to awareness?

Krishnamurti: Again let's be careful, let's be very clear that we are not asking this question with any motive. If there is a motive we are back in the trap of conditioned response. When the observer is wholly silent, not made silent, there is surely a different quality of awareness coming into being?

Questioner: What action could there possibly be in any circumstances without the observer—what question or what action?

Krishnamurti: Again, are you asking this question from this side of the river, or is it from the other bank? If you are on the other bank, you will not ask this question; if you are on that bank, your action will be from that bank. So there is an awareness of this bank, with all its structure, its nature and all its traps, and to try to escape from the trap is to fall into another trap. And what deadly monotony there is in all that! Awareness has shown us the nature of the trap, and therefore there is the negation of all traps; so the mind is now empty. It is empty of the "me" and of the trap. This mind has a different quality, a different dimension of awareness. This awareness is not aware that it is aware.

Questioner: My God, this is too difficult. You are saying things that seem true, that sound true, but I'm not there yet. Can you put it differently? Can you push me out of my trap?

Krishnamurti: Nobody can push you out of your trap—no guru, no drug, no mantra, nobody, including myself—nobody, especially myself. All that you have to do is to be aware from the beginning to the end, not become inattentive in the middle of it. This new quality of awareness is attention, and in this attention there is no frontier made by the "me". This attention is the highest form of virtue, therefore it is love. It is supreme intelligence, and there cannot be attention if you are not sensitive to the structure and the nature of these man-made traps.

IS THERE A GOD?

Questioner: I really would like to know if there is a god. If there isn't, life has no meaning. Not knowing god, man has invented him in a thousand beliefs and images. The division and the fear bred by all these beliefs have divided him from his fellow men. To escape the pain and the mischief of this division he creates yet more beliefs, and the mounting misery and confusion have engulfed him. Not knowing, we believe. Can I know god? I've asked this question of many saints both in India and here and they've all emphasised belief. "Believe and then you will know; without belief you can never know." What do you think?

Krishnamurti: Is belief necessary to find out? To learn is far more important than to know. Learning about belief is the end of belief. When the mind is free of belief then it can look. It is belief, or disbelief, that binds; for disbelief and belief are the same: they are the opposite sides of the same coin. So we can completely put aside positive or negative belief; the believer and the non-believer are the same. When this actually takes place then the question, "Is there a god?" has quite a different meaning. The word god with all its tradition, its memory, its intellectual and sentimental connotations—all this is not god. The word is not the real. So can the mind be free of the word?

Questioner: I don't know what that means.

Krishnamurti: The word is the tradition, the hope, the desire to find the absolute, the striving after the ultimate, the movement which gives vitality to existence. So the word itself becomes the

8

ultimate, yet we can see that the word is not the thing. The mind is the word, and the word is thought.

Questioner: And you're asking me to strip myself of the word? How can I do that? The word is the past; it is memory. The wife is the word, and the house is the word. In the beginning was the word. Also the word is the means of communication, identification. Your name is not you, and yet without your name I can't ask about you. And you're asking me if the mind can be free of the word—that is, can the mind be free of its own activity?

Krishnamurti: In the case of the tree the object is before our eyes, and the word refers to the tree by universal agreement. Now with the word god there is nothing to which it refers, so each man can create his own image of that for which there is no reference. The theologian does it in one way, the intellectual in another, and the believer and the non-believer in their own different ways. Hope generates this belief, and then seeking. This hope is the outcome of despair—the despair of all we see around us in the world. From despair hope is born; they also are two sides of the same coin. When there is no hope there is hell, and this fear of hell gives us the vitality of hope. Then illusion begins. So the word has led us to illusion and not to god at all. God is the illusion which we worship; and the non-believer creates the illusion of another god which he worships—the State, or some utopia, or some book which he thinks contains all truth. So we are asking you whether you can be free of the word with its illusion.

Questioner: I must meditate on this.

Krishnamurti: If there is no illusion, what is left?

Questioner: Only what is.

Krishnamurti: The "what is" is the most holy.

Questioner: If the "what is" is the most holy then war is most holy, and hatred, disorder, pain, avarice and plunder. Then we must not speak of any change at all. If "what is" is sacred, then every murderer and plunderer and exploiter can say, "Don't touch me, what I'm doing is sacred".

Krishnamurti: The very simplicity of that statement " 'what is' is most sacred", leads to great misunderstanding, because we don't see the truth of it. If you see that what *is* is sacred, you do not murder, you do not make war, you do not hope, you do not exploit. Having done these things you cannot claim immunity from a truth which you have violated. The white man who says to the black rioter, "What is is sacred, do not interfere, do not burn", has not seen, for if he had, the Negro would be sacred to him, and there would be no need to burn. So if each one of us sees this truth there must be change. This seeing of the truth is change.

Questioner: I came here to find out if there is god, and you have completely confused me.

Krishnamurti: You came to ask if there is god. We said: the word leads to illusion which we worship, and for this illusion we destroy each other willingly. When there is no illusion the "what is" is most sacred. Now let's look at what actually is. At a given moment the "what is" may be fear, or utter despair, or a fleeting joy. These things are constantly changing. And also there is the observer who says, "These things all change around me, but I remain permanent". Is that a fact, is that what really is? Is he not also changing, adding to and taking away from himself, modifying, adjusting himself, becoming or not becoming? So both the observer and the observed are constantly changing. *What is* is change. That is a fact. That *is* what is.

Questioner: Then is love changeable? If everything is a movement of change isn't love also part of that movement? And if love is changeable, then I can love one woman today and sleep with another tomorrow.

Krishnamurti: Is that love? Or are you saying that love is different from its expression? Or are you giving to expression greater importance than to love, and therefore making a contradiction and a conflict? Can love ever be caught in the wheel of change? If so then it can also be hate; then love is hate. It is only when there is no illusion that "what is" is most sacred. When there is no illusion "what is" is god or any other name that can be used. So god, or whatever name you give it, is when *you* are not. When you are, it is not. When you are not, love is. When you are, love is not.

FEAR

Questioner: I used to take drugs but now I am free of them. Why am I so frightened of everything? I wake up in the mornings paralysed with fear. I can hardly move out of bed. I'm frightened of going outside, and I'm frightened of being inside. Suddenly as I drive along this fear comes upon me, and I spend a whole day sweating, nervous, apprehensive, and at the end of the day I'm completely exhausted. Sometimes, though very rarely, in the company of a few intimate friends or at the house of my parents, I lose this fear; I feel quiet, happy, completely relaxed. As I came along in my car today, I was frightened of coming to see you, but as I came up the drive and walked to the door I suddenly lost this fear, and now as I sit here in this nice quiet room I feel so happy that I wonder what I was ever frightened about. Now I have no fear. I can smile and truthfully say: I'm very glad to see you! But I can't stay here for ever, and I know that when I leave here the cloud of fear will engulf me again. That is what I'm faced with. I've been to ever so many psychiatrists and analysts, both here and abroad, but they merely delve into my memories of childhood—and I'm fed up with it because the fear hasn't gone at all.

Krishnamurti: Let's forget childhood memories and all that nonsense, and come to the present. Here you are, and you say you are not frightened now; you're happy for the moment and can hardly imagine the fear you were in. Why have you no fear now? Is it the quiet, clear, well-proportioned room, furnished with good taste, and this sense of welcoming warmth which you feel? Is that why you are not frightened now?

Questioner: That's part of it. Also perhaps it is you. I heard you talk in Switzerland, and I've heard you here, and I feel a kind of deep friendship for you. But I don't want to depend on nice houses, welcoming atmospheres and good friends in order not to be afraid. When I go to my parents I have this same feeling of warmth. But it is deadly at home; all families are deadly with their little enclosed activities, their quarrels, and the vulgarity of all that loud talk about nothing, and their hypocrisy. I'm fed up with it all. And yet, when I go to them and there is this certain warmth, I *do* feel, for a while, free of this fear. The psychiatrists can't tell me what my fear is about. They call it a "floating fear". It's a black, bottomless, ghastly pit. I've spent a great deal of money and time on being analysed and it really hasn't helped at all. So what am I to *do*?

Krishnamurti: Is it that being sensitive you need a certain shelter, a certain security, and not being able to find it, you are frightened of the ugly world? Are you sensitive?

Questioner: Yes, I think so. Perhaps not in the way you mean, but I am sensitive. I don't like the noise, the bustle, the vulgarity of this modern existence and the way they throw sex at you everywhere you go today, and the whole business of fighting your way to some beastly little position. I am really frightened of all this —not that I can't fight and get a position for myself, but it makes me sick with fear.

Krishnamurti: Most people who are sensitive need a quiet shelter and a warm friendly atmosphere. Either they create it for themselves or depend on others who can give it to them—the family, the wife, the husband, the friend. Have you got such a friend?

Questioner: No. I'm frightened of having such a friend. I'm frightened of being dependent on him.

Krishnamurti: So there is this issue: being sensitive, demanding a certain shelter, and depending on others to give you that shelter. There is sensitivity, and dependence; the two often go together. And to depend on another is to fear losing him. So you depend more and more, and then the fear increases in proportion to your dependence. It is a vicious circle. Have you enquired why you depend? We depend on the postman, on physical comfort and so on; that's quite simple. We depend on people and things for our physical well-being and survival; it is quite natural and normal. We have to depend on what we may call the organisational side of society. But we also depend psychologically, and this dependence, though comforting, breeds fear. Why do we depend psychologically?

Questioner: You're talking to me about dependence now, but I came here to discuss fear.

Krishnamurti: Let's examine them both because they are inter-related as we shall see. Do you mind if we discuss them both? We were talking about dependence. What is dependence? Why does one psychologically depend on another? Isn't dependence the denial of freedom? Take away the house, the husband, the children, the possessions—what is a man if all these are removed? In himself he is insufficient, empty, lost. So out of this emptiness, of which he is afraid, he depends on property, on people and beliefs. You may be so sure of all the things you depend on that you can't imagine ever losing them— the love of your family, and the comfort. Yet fear continues. So we must be clear that any form of psychological dependence must inevitably breed fear, though the things you depend on may seem almost indestructible. Fear arises out of this inner insufficiency, poverty and emptiness. So now, do you see, we have three issues—sensitivity, dependence and fear? The three are inter-related. Take sensitivity: the more sensitive you are (unless you understand how to remain sensitive without dependence, how to be vulnerable without agony), the more you depend. Then take dependence: the more you depend, the more there is disgust and the demand to be free. This demand for freedom encourages fear, for this demand is a reaction, not freedom from dependence.

Questoner: Are you dependent on anything?

Krishnamurti: Of course I'm dependent physically on food, clothes and shelter, but psychologically, inwardly, I'm not dependent on anything—not on gods, not on social morality, not on belief, not on people. But it is irrelevant whether or not *I* am dependent. So, to continue: fear is the awareness of our inner emptiness, loneliness and poverty, and of not being able to do anything about it. We are concerned only with this fear which breeds dependence, and which is again increased by dependence. If we understand fear we also understand dependence. So to understand fear there must be sensitivity to discover, to understand how it comes into being. If one is at all sensitive one becomes conscious of one's own extraordinary emptiness—a bottomless pit which cannot be filled by the vulgar entertainment of drugs nor by the entertainment of the churches, nor the amusements of society: nothing can ever fill it. Knowing this the fear increases. This drives you to depend, and this dependence makes you more and more insensitive. And knowing this is so, you are frightened of it. So our question now is: how is one to go beyond this emptiness, this loneliness—not how is one to be self-sufficient, not how is one to camouflage this emptiness permanently?

Questioner: Why do you say it is not a question of becoming self-sufficient?

Krishnamurti: Because if you are self-sufficient you are no longer sensitive; you become smug and callous, indifferent and enclosed. To be without dependence, to go beyond dependence, doesn't mean to become self-sufficient. Can the mind face and live with this emptiness, and not escape in any diection?

Questioner: It would drive me mad to think I had to live with it forever.

Krishnamurti: Any movement away from this emptiness is an escape. And this flight away from something, away from "what is", is fear. Fear is flight away from something. What *is* is not the fear; it is the *flight* which is the fear, and *this* will drive you mad, not the emptiness itself. So what is this emptiness, this loneliness? How does it come about? Surely it comes through comparison and measurement, doesn't it? I compare myself with the saint, the master, the great musician, the man who knows, the man who has arrived. In this comparison I find myself wanting and insufficient: I have no talent, I am inferior, I have not "realised"; I am not, and that man is. So out of measurement and comparison comes the enormous cavity of emptiness and nothingness. And the flight from this cavity is fear. And the fear stops us from understanding this bottomless pit. It is a neurosis which feeds upon itself. And again, this measurement, this comparison, is the very essence of dependence. So we are back again at dependence, a vicious circle.

Questioner: We have come a long way in this discussion and things are clearer. There is dependence; is it possible not to depend? Yes, I think it is possible. Then we have the fear; is it possible not to run away from emptiness at all, which means, not to escape through fear? Yes, I think it is possible. That means we are left with the emptiness. Is it possible then to face this emptiness since we have stopped running away from it through fear? Yes, I think it is possible. Is it possible finally, not to measure, not to compare? For if we have come this far, and I think we have, only this emptiness remains, and one sees that this emptiness is the outcome of comparison. And one sees that dependence and fear are the outcome of this emptiness. So there is comparison, emptiness, fear, dependence. Can I really live a life without comparison, without measurement?

Krishnamurti: Of course you have to measure to put a carpet on the floor!

Questioner: Yes. I mean can I live without psychological comparison?

Krishnamurti: Do you know what it means to live without psychological comparison when all your life you have been conditioned to compare—at school, at games, at the University and in the office? Everything is comparison. To live without comparison! Do you know what it means? It means no dependence, no self-sufficiency, no seeking, no asking; therefore it means to love. Love has no comparison, and so love has no fear. Love is not aware of itself as love, for the word is not the thing.

HOW TO LIVE IN THIS WORLD

Questioner: Please, Sir, could you tell me how I am to live in this world? I don't want to be part of it yet I have to live in it, I have to have a house and earn my own living. And my neighbours are of this world; my children play with theirs, and so one becomes a part of this ugly mess, whether one wants to or not. I want to find out how to live in this world without escaping from it, without going into a monastery or around the world in a sailing boat. I want to educate my children differently, but first I want to know how to live surrounded by so much violence, greed, hypocrisy, competition and brutality.

Krishnamurti: Don't let's make a problem of it. When anything becomes a problem we are caught in the solution of it, and then the problem becomes a cage, a barrier to further exploration and understanding. So don't let us reduce all life to a vast and complex problem. If the question is put in order to overcome the society in which we live, or to find a substitute for that society, or to try to escape from it though living in it, it must inevitably lead to a contradictory and hypocritical life. This question also implies, doesn't it, the complete denial of ideology? If you are really enquiring you cannot start with a conclusion, and all ideologies are a conclusion. So we must begin by finding out what you mean by living.

Questioner: Please, Sir, let's go step by step.

Krishnamurti: I am very glad that we can go into this step by step, patiently, with an enquiring mind and heart. Now what do you mean by living?

Questioner: I've never tried to put it into words. I'm bewildered, I don't know what to do, how to live. I've lost faith in everything —religions, philosophies and political utopias. There is war between individuals and between nations. In this permissive society everything is allowed—killing, riots, the cynical oppression of one country by another, and nobody does anything about it because interference might mean world war. I am faced with all this and I don't know what to do; I don't know how to live at all. I don't want to live in the midst of such confusion.

Krishnamurti: What is it you are asking for—a different life, or for a new life which comes about with the understanding of the old life? If you want to live a different life without understanding what has brought about this confusion, you will always be in contradiction, in conflict, in confusion. And that of course is not a new life at all. So are you asking for a new life or for a modified continuity of the old one, or to understand the old one?

Questioner: I'm not at all sure what I want, but I am beginning to see what I don't want.

Krishnamurti: Is what you don't want based on your free understanding or on your pleasure and pain? Are you judging out of your revolt, or do you see the causation of this conflict and misery, and, because you see it, reject it?

Questioner: You're asking me too many things. All I know is that I want to live a different kind of life. I don't know what it means; I don't know why I'm seeking it; and, as I said, I'm utterly bewildered by it all.

Krishnamurti: Your basic question is, isn't it, how are you to live in this world? Before you find out let us first see what this world is. The world is not only all that surrounds us, it is also our relationship to all these things and people, to ourselves, to ideas. That is, our relationship to property, to people, to concepts—in fact our relationship to the stream of events which we call life. This is the world. We see division into nationalities, into religious, economic, political, social and ethnical groups; the whole world is broken up and is as fragmented outwardly as its human beings are inwardly. In fact, this outer fragmentation is the manifestation of the human being's inner division.

Questioner: Yes, I see this fragmentation very clearly, and I am also beginning to see that the human being is responsible.

Krishnamurti: You are the human being!

Questioner: Then can I live differently from what I am myself? I'm suddenly realising that if I am to live in a totally different way there must be a new birth in me, a new mind and heart, new eyes. And I realise also that this hasn't happened. I live the way I am, and the way I am has made life as it is. But where does one go from there?

Krishnamurti: You don't go anywhere from there! There is no going anywhere. The going, or the searching for the ideal, for what we think is better, gives us a feeling that we are progressing, that we are moving towards a better world. But this movement is no movement at all because the end has been projected out of our misery, confusion, greed and envy. So this end, which is supposed to be the opposite of what is, is really the same as what is, it is engendered by what is. Therefore it creates the conflict between what is and what should be. This is where our basic confusion and conflict arises. The end is not over there, not on the other side of the wall; the beginning and the end are here.

Questioner: Wait a minute, Sir, please; I don't understand this at all. Are you telling me that the ideal of what should be is the result of not understanding what is? Are you telling me that what should be *is* what is, and that this movement from what is to what should be isn't really a movement at all?

Krishnamurti: It is an idea; it is fiction. If you understand what is, what need is there for what should be?

Questioner: Is that so? I understand what is. I understand the bestiality of war, the horror of killing, and because I understand it I have this ideal of not killing. The ideal is born out of my understanding of what is, therefore it is not an escape.

Krishnamurti: If you understand that killing is terrible do you have to have an ideal in order not to kill? Perhaps we are not clear about the word understanding. When we say we understand something, in that is implied, isn't it, that we have learnt all it has to say? We have explored it and discovered the truth or the falseness of it. This implies also, doesn't it, that this understanding is not an intellectual affair, but that one has felt it deeply in one's heart? There is understanding only when the mind and the heart are in perfect harmony. Then one says, "I have understood this, and finished with it", and it no longer has the vitality to breed further conflict. Do we both give the same meaning to that word understand?

Questioner: I hadn't before, but now I see that what you are saying is true. Yet I honestly don't understand, in that way, the total disorder of the world, which, as you so rightly pointed out, is my own disorder. How can I understand it? How can I completely learn about the disorder, the entire disorder and confusion of the world, and of myself?

Krishnamurti: Do not use the word how, please.

Questioner: Why not?

Krishnamurti: The how implies that somebody is going to give you a method, a recipe, which, if you practise it, will bring about understanding. Can understanding ever come about through a method? Understanding means love and the sanity of the mind. And love cannot be practised or taught. The sanity of the mind can only come about when there is clear perception, seeing things as they are unemotionally, not sentimentally. Neither of these two things can be taught by another, nor by a system invented by yourself or by another.

Questioner: You are too persuasive, Sir, or is it perhaps that you are too logical? Are you trying to influence me to see things as you see them?

Krishnamurti: God forbid! Influence in any form is destructive of love. Propaganda to make the mind sensitive, alert, will only make it dull and insensitive. So we are in no way trying to influence you or persuade you, or make you depend. We are only pointing out, exploring together. And to explore together you must be free, both of me and of your own prejudices and fears. Otherwise you go round and round in circles. So we must go back to our original question: how am I to live in this world? To live in this world we must deny the world. By that we mean: deny the ideal, the war, the fragmentation, the competition, the envy and so on. We don't mean deny the world as a schoolboy revolts against his parents. We mean deny it because we understand it. This understanding is negation.

Questioner: I am out of my depth.

Krishnamurti: You said you do not want to live in the confusion, the dishonesty and ugliness of this world. So you deny it. But from what background do you deny it, why do you deny it? Do you deny it because you want to live a peaceful life, a life of complete security and enclosure, or do you deny it because you see what it actually is?

Questioner: I think I deny it because I see around me what is taking place. Of course my prejudices and fear are also involved. So it is a mixture of what is actually taking place and my own anxiety.

Krishnamurti: Which predominates, your own anxiety or the actual seeing of what is around you? If fear predominates, then you can't see what is actually going on around you, because fear is darkness, and in darkness you can see absolutely nothing. If you realise that, then you can see the world actually as it is, then you can see yourself actually as you are. Because you are the world, and the world is you; they are not two separate entities.

Questioner: Would you please explain more fully what you mean by the world is me and I am the world?

Krishnamurti: Does this really need explaining? Do you want me to describe in detail what you are and show you that it is the same as what the world is? Will this description convince you that you are the world? Will you be convinced by a logical, sequential explanation showing you the cause and the effect? If you are convinced by careful description, will that give you understanding? Will it make you feel that you are the world, make you feel responsible for the world? It seems so clear that our human greed, envy, aggression and violence have brought about the society in which we live, a legalised acceptance of what we are. I think this is really sufficiently clear and let's not spend any more time on this issue. You see, we don't feel this, we don't love, therefore there is this division between me and the world.

Questioner: May I come back again tomorrow?

* * *

He came back the next day eagerly, and there was the bright light of enquiry in his eyes.

Questioner: I want, if you are willing, to go further into this question of how I am to live in this world. I do now understand, with my heart and my mind, as you explained yesterday, the utter unimportance of ideals. I had quite a long struggle with it and have come to see the triviality of ideals. You are saying, aren't you, that when there are no ideals or escapes there is only the past, the thousand yesterdays which make up the me? So when I ask, "How am I to live in this world?" I have not only put a wrong question, but I have also made a contradictory statement, for I have placed the world and the "me" in opposition to each other. And this contradiction is what I call living. So when I ask the question, "How am I to live in this world?" I am really trying to improve this contradiction, to justify it, to modify it, because that's all I know; I don't know anything else.

Krishnamurti: This then is the question we have now: must living always be in the past, must all activity spring from the past, is all relationship the outcome of the past, is living the complex memory of the past? That is all we know—the past modifying the present. And the future is the outcome of this past acting through the present. So the past, the present and the future are all the past. And this past is what we call living. The mind is the past, the brain is the past, the feelings are the past, and action coming from these is the positive activity of the known. This whole process is your life and all the relationship and activity that you know. So when you ask how you are to live in this world you are asking for a change of prisons.

Questioner: I don't mean that. What I mean is: I see very clearly that my process of thinking and doing is the past working through the present to the future. This is all I know, and that's a fact. And I realise that unless there is a change in this structure I am caught in it, I am of it. From this the question inevitably arises: how am I to change?

Krishnamurti: To live in this world sanely there must be a radical change of the mind and of the heart.

Questioner: Yes, but what do you mean by change? How am I to change if whatever I do is the movement of the past? I can only change myself, nobody else can change me. And I don't see what it means—to change.

Krishnamurti: So the question, "How am I to live in this world?" has now become, "How am I to change?"—bearing in mind that the how doesn't mean a method, but is an enquiry to understand. What is change? Is there any change at all? Or can you ask whether there is any change at all only *after* there has been a total change and revolution? Let's begin again to find out what this word means. Change implies a movement from what is to something different. Is this something different merely an opposite, or does it belong to a different order altogether? If it is merely an opposite then it is not different at all, because all opposites are mutually dependent, like hot and cold, high and low. The opposite is contained within, and determined by, its opposite; it exists only in comparison, and things that are comparative have different measures of the same quality, and therefore they are similar. So change to an opposite is no change at all. Even if this going towards what seems different gives you the feeling that you are really doing something, it is an illusion.

Questioner: Let me absorb this for a moment.

Krishnamurti: So what are we concerned with now? Is it possible to bring about in ourselves the birth of a new order altogether that is not related to the past? The past is irrelevant to this enquiry, and trivial, because it is irrelevant to the new order.

Questioner: How can you say it is trivial and irrelevant? We've been saying all along that the past is the issue, and now you say it is irrelevant.

Krishnamurti: The past seems to be the only issue because it is the only thing that holds our minds and hearts. It alone is important to us. But why do we give importance to it? Why is this little space all-important? If you are totally immersed in it, utterly committed to it, then you will never listen to change. The man who is *not* wholly committed is the only one capable of listening, enquiring and asking. Only then will he be able to see the triviality of this little space. So, are you completely immersed, or is your head above the water? If your head is above the water then you can see that this little thing is trivial. Then you have room to look around. How deeply are you immersed? Nobody can answer this for you except yourself. In the very asking of this question there is already freedom and, therefore, one is not afraid. Then your vision is extensive. When this pattern of the past holds you completely by the throat, then you acquiesce, accept, obey, follow, believe. It is only when you are aware that this is not freedom that you are starting to climb out of it. So we are again asking: what is change, what is revolution? Change is not a movement from the known to the known, and all political revolutions are that. This kind of change is not what we are talking about. To progress from being a sinner to being a saint is to progress from one illusion to another. So now we are free of change as a movement from this to that.

Questioner: Have I really understood this? What am I to do with anger, violence and fear when they arise in me? Am I to give them free reign? How am I to deal with them? There must be change there, otherwise I am what I was before.

Krishnamurti: Is it clear to you that these things cannot be overcome by their opposites? If so, you have only the violence, the envy, the anger, the greed. The feeling arises as the result of a challenge, and then it is named. This naming of the feeling re-establishes it in the old pattern. If you do not name it, which means you do not identify yourself with it, then the feeling is new and it will go away by itself. The naming of it strengthens it and gives it a continuity which is the whole process of thought.

Questioner: I am being driven into a corner where I see myself actually as I am, and I see how trivial I am. From there what comes next?

Krishnamurti: Any movement from what I am strengthens what I am. So change *is no movement at all*. Change is the denial of change, and now only can I put this question: is there a change at all? This question can be put only when all movement of thought has come to an end, for thought must be denied for the beauty of non-change. In the total negation of all movement of thought away from what is, is the ending of what is.

RELATIONSHIP

Questioner: I have come a long way to see you. Although I am married and have children I have been away from them, wandering, meditating, as a mendicant. I have puzzled greatly over this very complicated problem of relationship. When I go into a village and they give me food, I am related to the giver, as I am related to my wife and children. In another village when somebody gives me clothes I am related to the whole factory that produced them. I am related to the earth on which I walk, to the tree under which I take shelter, to everything. And yet I am alone, isolated. When I am with my wife, I am separate even during sex—it is an act of separation. When I go into a temple it is still the worshipper being related to the thing he worships: separation again. So in all relationships, as I see it, there is this separation, duality, and behind or through it, or around it, there is a peculiar sense of unity. When I see the beggar it hurts me, for I am like him and I feel as he feels—lonely, desperate, sick, hungry. I feel for him, and with him, for his meaningless existence. Some rich man comes along in his big motor-car and give me a lift, but I feel uncomfortable in his company, yet at the same time I feel for him and am related to him. So I have meditated upon this strange phenomenon of relationship. Can we on this lovely morning, overlooking this deep valley, talk over together this question?

Krishnamurti: Is all relationship out of this isolation? Can there be relationship so long as there is any separateness, division? Can there be relationship if there is no contact, not only physical but at every level of our being, with another? One may hold the hand of another and yet be miles away, wrapped in one's own thoughts and problems. One may be in a group and yet be painfully alone. So one asks: can there be any kind of relationship with the tree, the flower, the human being, or with the skies and the lovely sunset, when the mind in its activities is isolating itself? And can there be any contact ever, with anything at all, even when the mind is *not* isolating itself?

Questioner: Everything and everybody has its own existence. Everything and everybody is shrouded in its own existence. I can never penetrate this enclosure of another's being. However much I love someone, his existence is separate from mine. I can perhaps touch him from the outside, mentally or physically, but his existence is his own, and mine is forever on the outside of it. Similarly he cannot reach me. Must we always remain two separate entities, each in his own world, with his own limitations, within the prison of his own consciousness?

Krishnamurti: Each lives within his own tissue, you in yours, he in his. And is there any possibility, ever, of breaking through this tissue? Is this tissue—this shroud, this envelope—the word? Is it made up of your concern with yourself and his with himself, your desires opposed to his? Is this capsule the past? It is all of this, isn't it? It isn't one particular thing but a whole bundle which the mind carries about. You have your burden, another has his. Can these burdens ever be dropped so that the mind meets the mind, the heart meets the heart? This is really the question, isn't it?

Questioner: Even if all these burdens are dropped, if that were possible, even then he remains in his skin with his thoughts, and I in mine with my thoughts. Sometimes the gap is narrow, sometimes it is wide, but we are always two separate islands. The gap seems to be widest when we care most about it and try to bridge it.

Krishnamurti: You can identify yourself with that villager or with that flaming bougainvillea—which is a mental trick to pretend unity. Identification with something is one of the most hypocritical states—to identify oneself with a nation, with a belief and yet remain alone is a favourite trick to cheat loneliness. Or you identify yourself so completely with your belief that you are that belief, and this is a neurotic state. Now let's put away this urge to be identified with a person or an idea or a thing. That way there is no harmony, unity or love. So our next question is: can you tear through the envelope so that there is no more envelope? Then only would there be a possibility of total contact. How is one to tear through the envelope? The "how" doesn't mean a method, but rather an enquiry which might open the door.

Questioner: Yes, no other contact can be called relationship at all, though we say it is.

Krishnamurti: Do we tear the envelope bit by bit or cut through it immediately? If we tear it bit by bit, which is what analysts sometimes claim to do, the job is never done. It is not through time that you can break down this separation.

Questioner: Can I enter into the envelope of another? And isn't his envelope his very existence, his heartbeats and his blood, his feelings and his memories?

Krishnamurti: Are *you* not the very envelope itself?

Questioner: Yes.

Krishnamurti: The very movement to tear through the other envelope, or extend outside of your own, is the very affirmation and the action of your own envelope: you are the envelope. So you are the observer of the envelope, and you are also the envelope itself. In this case you are the observer and the observed: so is he, and that's how we remain. And you try to reach him and he tries to reach you. Is this possible? You are the island surrounded by seas, and he is also the island surrounded by seas. You see that you are both the island and the sea; there is no division between them; you are the entire earth with the sea. Therefore there is no division as the island and the sea. The other person doesn't see this. He is the island surrounded by sea; he tries to reach you, or, if you are foolish enough, you may try to reach him. Is that possible? How can there be a contact between a man who is free and another who is bound? Since you are the observer and the observed, you are the whole movement of the earth and the sea. But the other, who doesn't understand this, is still the island surrounded by water. He tries to reach you, and is everlastingly failing because he maintains his insularity. It is only when he leaves it and is, like you, open to the movement of the skies, the earth, and the sea, that there can be contact. The one who sees that the barrier is himself can no longer have a barrier. Therefore he, in himself, is not separate at all. The other has not seen that the barrier is himself and so maintains the belief in his separateness. How can this man reach the other? It is not possible.

* * *

Questioner: If we may I should like to continue from where we left off yesterday. You were saying that the mind is the maker of the envelope around itself, and that this envelope is the mind. I really don't understand this. Intellectually I can agree, but the nature of perception eludes me. I should like very much to understand it—not verbally but actually feel it—so that there is no conflict in my life.

Krishnamurti: There is the space between what the mind calls the envelope which it has made, and itself. There is the space between the ideal and the action. In these different fragmentations of space between the observer and the observed, or between different things it observes, is all conflict and struggle, and all the problems of life. There is the separation between this envelope around me and the envelope around another. In that space is all our existence, all our relationship and battle.

Questioner. When you talk of the division between the observer and the observed do you mean these fragmentations of space in our thinking and in our daily actions?

Krishnamurti: What is this space? There is the space between you and your envelope, the space between him and his envelope, and there is the space between the two envelopes. These spaces all appear to the observer. What are these spaces made of? How do they come into being? What is the quality and the nature of these divided spaces? If we could remove these fragmentary spaces what would happen?

Questioner: There would then be true contact on all levels of one's being.

Krishnamurti: Is that all?

Questioner: There would be no more conflict, for all conflict is relationship across these spaces.

Krishnamurti: Is that all? When this space actually disappears— not verbally or intellectually—but actually disappears—there is complete harmony, unity, between you and him, between you and another. In this harmony you and he cease and there is only this vast space which can never be broken up. The small structure of the mind comes to an end, for the mind is fragmentation.

Questioner: I really can't understand this at all, though I have a deep feeling within me that it is so. I can see that when there is love this actually takes place, but I don't know that love. It's not with me all the time. It is not in my heart. I see it only as if through a misty glass. I can't honestly grasp it with all my being. Could we, as you suggested, consider what these spaces are made of, how they come into being?

Krishnamurti: Let's be quite sure that we both understand the same thing when we use the word space. There is the physical space between people and things, and there is the psychological space between people and things. Then there is also the space between the idea and the actual. So all this, the physical and the psychological, is space, more or less limited and defined. We are *not* now talking of the physical space. We are talking of the psychological space between people and the psychological space in the human being himself, in his thoughts and activities. How does this space come about? Is it fictitious, illusory, or is it real? Feel it, be aware of it, make sure you haven't just got a mental image of it, bear in mind that the description is never the thing. Be quite sure that you know what we are talking about. Be quite aware that this limited space, this division, exists in you: don't move from there if you don't understand. Now how does this space come about?

Questioner: We see the physical space between things. . . .

Krishnamurti: Don't explain anything; just feel your way into it. We are asking how this space has come into being. Don't give an explanation or a cause, but remain with this space and feel it. Then the cause and the description will have very little meaning and no value. This space has come into being because of thought, which is the "me", the word—which is the whole division. Thought itself is this distance, this division. Thought is always breaking itself up into fragments and creating division. Thought always cuts up what it observes into fragments within space—as you and me, yours and mine, me and my thoughts, and so on. This space, which thought has created between what it observes, has become real; and it is this space that divides. Then thought tries to build a bridge over this division, thus playing a trick upon itself all the time, deceiving itself and hoping for unity.

Questioner: That reminds me of the old statement about thought: it is a thief disguising himself as a policeman in order to catch the thief.

Krishnamurti: Don't bother to quote, Sir, however ancient it is. We are considering what actually is going on. In seeing the truth of the nature of thought and its activities, thought becomes quiet. Thought being quiet, not made quiet, is there space?

Questioner: It is thought itself which now rushes in to answer this question.

Krishnamurti: Exactly! Therefore we do not even ask the question. The mind now is completely harmonious, without fragmentation; the little space has ceased and there is only space. When the mind is completely quiet there is the vastness of space and silence.

Questioner: So I begin to see that my relationship to another is between thought and thought; whatever I answer is the noise of thought, and realising it, I am silent.

Krishnamurti: This silence is the benediction.

CONFLICT

Questioner: I find myself in a great deal of conflict with everything about me; and also everything within me is in conflict. People have spoken of divine order; nature is harmonious; it seems that man is the only animal who violates this order, making so much misery for others and for himself. When I wake up in the morning I see from my window little birds fighting with each other, but they soon separate and fly away, whereas I carry this war with myself and with others inside me all the time; there is no escaping it. I wonder if I can ever be at peace with myself. I must say I should like to find myself in complete harmony with everything about me and with myself. As one sees from this window the quiet sea and the light on the water, one has a feeling deep within oneself that there must be a way of living without these endless quarrels with oneself and with the world. Is there any harmony at all, anywhere? Or is there only everlasting disorder? If there is harmony, at what level can it exist? Or does it only exist on the top of some mountain which the burning valleys can never know?

Krishnamurti: Can one go from one to the other? Can one change that which is to that which is not? Can disharmony be transformed into harmony?

Questioner: Is conflict necessary then? It may perhaps, after all, be the natural order of things.

Krishnamurti: If one accepted that, one would have to accept everything society stands for: wars, ambitious competition, an aggressive way of life—all the brutal violence of men, inside and outside of his so-called holy places. Is this natural? Will this bring about any unity? Wouldn't it be better for us to consider these two facts—the fact of conflict with all its complicated struggles, and the fact of the mind demanding order, harmony, peace, beauty, love?

Questioner: I know nothing about harmony. I see it in the heavens, in the seasons, in the mathematical order of the universe. But that doesn't give me order in my own heart and mind; the absolute order of mathematics is not *my* order. I have no order, I am in deep disorder. I know there are different theories of gradual evolution towards the so-called perfection of political utopias and religious heavens, but this leaves me where I actually am. The world may perhaps be perfect in ten thousand years from now, but in the meantime I'm having hell.

Krishnamurti: We see the disorder in ourselves and in society. Both are very complex. There are really no answers. One can examine all this very carefully, analyse it closely, look for causes of disorder in oneself and in society, expose them to the light and perhaps believe that one will free the mind from them. This analytical process is what most people are doing, intelligently or unintelligently, and it doesn't get anybody very far. Man has analysed himself for thousands of years, and produced no result but literature! The many saints have paralysed themselves in concepts and ideological prisons; they too are in conflict. The cause of our conflict is this everlasting duality of desire: the endless corridor of the opposites creating envy, greed, ambition, aggression, fear, and all the rest of it. Now I wonder if there isn't an altogether different approach to this problem? The acceptance of this struggle and all our efforts to get out of it have become traditional. The whole approach is traditional. In this traditional approach the mind operates but, as we see, the traditional approach of the mind creates more disorder. So the problem is not how to end disorder, but rather whether the mind can look at it freed from tradition. And then perhaps there may be no problem at all.

Questioner: I don't follow you at all.

Krishnamurti: There is this fact of disorder. There is no doubt about it: it is an actual fact. The traditional approach to this fact is to analyse it, to try to discover the cause of it and overcome the cause, or else to invent its opposite and battle towards that. This is the traditional approach with its disciplines, drills, controls, suppressions, sublimations. Man has done this for thousands upon thousands of years; it has led nowhere. Can we abandon this approach completely and look at the problem entirely differently—that is, not try to go beyond it, or to resolve it, or to overcome it, or to escape from it? Can the mind do this?

Questioner: Perhaps. . . .

Krishnamurti: Don't answer so quickly! This is a tremendous thing I am asking you. From the beginning of time man has tried to deal with all his problems, either by going beyond them, resolving them, overcoming them or escaping from them. Please do not think you can push all that aside so lightly, simply with a verbal agreement. It makes up the very structure of everybody's mind. Can the mind now, understanding all this non-verbally, actually free itself from the tradition? This traditional way of dealing with the conflict never solves it, but only adds more conflict: being violent, which is conflict, I add the additional conflict of trying to become non-violent. All social morality and all religious prescriptions are that. Are we together?

Questioner: Yes.

Krishnamurti: Then do you see how far we have come? Having, through understanding, repudiated all these traditional approaches, what is the actual state of the mind now? Because the state of the mind is far more important than the conflict itself.

Questioner: I really don't know.

Krishnamurti: Why don't you know? Why aren't you aware, if you have really abandoned the traditional approach, of the state of your mind? Why don't you know? Either you have abandoned it or you haven't. If you have, you would know it. If you have, then your mind is made innocent to look at the problem. You can look at the problem as though for the first time. And if you do this, *is* there a problem of conflict at all? Because you look at the problem with the old eyes it is not only strengthened but also moves in its well-worn path. So what is important is how you look at the problem—whether you look at it with new eyes or old eyes. The new eyes are freed from the conditioned responses to the problem. Even to name the problem through recognition is to approach it in the traditional way. Justification, condemnation, or translation of the problem in terms of pleasure and pain, are all involved in this habitual traditional approach of doing something about it. This is generally called positive action with regard to the problem. But when the mind brushes all that aside as being ineffectual, unintelligent, then it has become highly sensitive, highly ordered, and free.

Questioner: You're asking too much of me, I can't do it. I'm incapable of it. You're asking me to be super-human!

Krishnamurti: You're making difficulties for yourself, blocking yourself, when you say you must become super-human. It's nothing of the kind. You keep on looking at things with eyes that want to interfere, that want to do something about what they see. Stop doing anything about it, for whatever you do belongs to the traditional approach. That's all. Be simple. This is the miracle of perception—to perceive with a heart and mind that are completely cleansed of the past. Negation is the most positive action.

THE RELIGIOUS LIFE

Questioner: I should like to know what a religious life is. I have stayed in monasteries for several months, meditated, lead a disciplined life, read a great deal. I've been to various temples, churches and mosques. I've tried to lead a very simple, harmless life, trying not to hurt people or animals. This surely isn't all there is to a religious life? I've practised yoga, studied Zen and followed many religious disciplines. I am, and have always been, a vegetarian. As you see, I'm getting old now, and I've lived with some of the saints in different parts of the world, but somehow I feel that all this is only the outskirts of the real thing. So I wonder if we can discuss today what to you is a religious life.

Krishnamurti: A sannyasi came to see me one day and he was sad. He said he had taken a vow of celibacy and left the world to become a mendicant, wandering from village to village, but his sexual desires were so imperious that one morning he decided to have his sexual organs surgically removed. For many months he was in constant pain, but somehow it healed, and after many years he fully realised what he had done. And so he came to see me and in that little room he asked me what he could do now, having mutilated himself, to become normal again—not physically, of course, but inwardly. He had done this thing because sexual activity was considered contrary to a religious life. It was considered mundane, belonging to the world of pleasure, which a real sannyasi must at all costs avoid. He said, "Here I am, feeling completely lost, deprived of my man-

38

hood. I struggled so hard against my sexual desires, trying to control them, and ultimately this terrible thing took place. Now what am I to do? I know that what I did was wrong. My energy has almost gone and I seem to be ending my life in darkness." He held my hand, and we sat silently for some time.

Is this a religious life? Is the denial of pleasure or beauty a way that leads to a religious life? To deny the beauty of the skies and the hills and the human form, will that lead to a religious life? But that is what most saints and monks believe. They torture themselves in that belief. Can a tortured, twisted, distorted mind ever find what is a religous life? Yet all religions assert that the only way to reality or to God, or whatever they call it, is through this torture, this distortion. They all make the distinction between what they call a spiritual or religious life and what they call a worldly life.

A man who lives only for pleasure, with occasional flashes of sorrow and piety, whose whole life is given to amusement and entertainment is, of course, a worldly man, although he may also be very clever, very scholarly, and fill his life with other people's thoughts or his own. And a man who has a gift and exercises it for the benefit of society, or for his own pleasure, and who achieves fame in the fulfilment of that gift, such a man, surely, is also worldly. But it is also worldly to go to church, or to the temple or the mosque, to pray, steeped in prejudice, bigotry, utterly unaware of the brutality that this implies. It is worldly to be patriotic, nationalistic, idealistic. The man who shuts himself up in a monastery—getting up at regular hours with a book in hand, reading and praying—is surely also worldly. And the man who goes out to do good works, whether he is a social reformer or a missionary, is just like the politician in his concern with the world. The division between the religious life and the world is the very essence of worldliness. The minds of all these people—monks, saints, reformers—are not very different from the minds of those who are only concerned with the things that give pleasure.

So it is important not to divide life into the worldly and the non-worldly. It is important not to make the distinction between the worldly and the so-called religious. Without the world of matter, the material world, we wouldn't be here. Without the beauty of the sky and the single tree on the hill, without that woman going by and that man riding the horse, life wouldn't be possible. We are concerned with the totality of life not a particular part of it which is considered religious in opposition to the rest. So one begins to see that a religious life is concerned with the whole and not with the particular.

Questioner: I understand what you say. We have to deal with the totality of living; we can't separate the world from the so-called spirit. So the question is: in what way can we act religiously with regard to all the things in life?

Krishnamurti: What do we mean by acting religiously? Don't you mean a way of life in which there is no division—division between the worldly and the religious, between what should be and what shouldn't be, between me and you, between like and dislike? This division is conflict. A life of conflict is not a religious life. A religious life is only possible when we deeply understand conflict. This understanding is intelligence. It is this intelligence that acts rightly. What most people call intelligence is merely deftness in some technical activity, or cunning in business or political chicanery.

Questioner: So my question really means, how is one to live without conflict, and bring about that feeling of true sanctity which is not simply emotional piety conditioned by some religious cage—no matter how old and venerated that cage is?

Krishnamurti: A man living without too much conflict in a village, or dreaming in a cave on a "sacred" hillside, is surely not living the religious life that we are talking about. To end conflict is one of the most complex things. It needs self-observation and the sensitivity of awareness of the outer as well as of the inner. Conflict can only end when there is the understanding of the contradiction in oneself. This contradiction will always exist if there is no freedom from the known, which is the past. Freedom from the past means living in the now which is not of time, in which there is only this movement of freedom, untouched by the past, by the known.

Questioner: What do you mean by freedom from the past?

Krishnamurti: The past is all our accumulated memories. These memories act in the present and create our hopes and fears of the future. These hopes and fears *are* the psychological future; without them there is no future. So the present is the action of the past, and the mind is this movement of the past. The past acting in the present creates what we call the future. This response of the past is involuntary, it is not summoned or invited, it is upon us before we know it.

Questioner: In that case, how are we going to be free of it?

Krishnamurti: To be aware of this movement without choice— because choice again is more of this same movement of the past —is to observe the past in action: such observation is *not* a movement of the past. To observe without the image of thought is action in which the past has ended. To observe the tree without thought is action without the past. To observe the action of the past is again action without the past. The state of seeing is more important than what is seen. To be aware of the past in that choiceless observation is not only to act differently, but to be different. In this awareness memory acts without impediment, and efficiently. To be religious is to be so choicelessly aware that there is freedom from the known even whilst the known acts wherever it has to.

Questioner: But the known, the past, still sometimes acts even when it should not; it still acts to cause conflict.

Krishnamurti: To be aware of this is also to be in a state of inaction with regard to the past which is acting. So freedom from the known is truly the religious life. That doesn't mean to wipe out the known but to enter a different dimension altogether from which the known is observed. This action of seeing choicelessly is the action of love. The religious life is this action, and all living is this action, and the religious mind is this action. So religion, and the mind, and life, and love, are one.

SEEING THE WHOLE

Questioner: When I listen to you I seem to understand what you are talking about, not only verbally, but at a much deeper level. I am part of it; I fully grasp with my whole being the truth of what you say. My hearing is sharpened, and the very seeing of the flowers, the trees, and those mountains with snow, makes me feel I am part of them. In this awareness I have no conflict, no contradiction. It is as though I could do anything, and that whatever I did would be true, would not bring either conflict or pain. But unfortunately that state doesn't last. Perhaps it lasts for an hour or two while I'm listening to you. When I leave the talks it all seems to evaporate and I'm back where I was. I try to be aware of myself; I keep remembering the state I was in when I listened to your talks, keep trying to reach it, hold on to it, and this becomes a struggle. You have said, "Be aware of your conflict, listen to your conflict, see the causes of your conflict, your conflict is yourself". I am aware of my conflict, my pain, my sorrow, my confusion, but this awareness in no way resolves these things. On the contrary, being aware of them seems to give them vitality and duration. You talk of choiceless awareness, which again breeds another battle in me, for I am full of choice, decisions and opinions. I have applied this awareness to a particular habit I have, and it has not gone. When you are aware of some conflict or strain, this same awareness keeps looking to see if it has already gone. And this seems to remind you of it, and you never shake it off.

Krishnamurti: Awareness is not a commitment to something. Awareness is an observation, both outer and inner, in which direction has stopped. You are aware, but the thing of which you are aware is not being encouraged or nourished. Awareness is not concentration on something. It is not an action of the will chosing what it will be aware of, and analysing it to bring about a certain result. When awareness is deliberately focussed on a particular object, as a conflict, that is the action of will which is concentration. When you concentrate—that is, put all your energy and thought within your chosen frontiers, whether reading a book or watching your anger—then, in this exclusion, the thing you are concentrating upon is strengthened, nourished. So here we have to understand the nature of awareness: we have to understand what we are talking about when we use the word awareness. Now, you can either be aware of a particular thing, or be aware of that particular as part of the total. The particular by itself has very little meaning, but when you see the total, then that particular has a relationship to the whole. Only in this relationship does the particular have its right meaning; it doesn't become all-important, it is not exaggerated. So the real question is: does one see the total process of life or is one concentrated on the particular, thus missing the whole field of life? To be aware of the whole field is to see also the particular, but, at the same time, to understand its relationship to the whole. If you are angry and are concerned with ending that anger, then you focus your attention on the anger and the whole escapes you and the anger is strengthened. But anger is inter-related to the whole. So when we separate the particular from the whole, the particular breeds its own problems.

Questioner: What do you mean by seeing the whole? What is this totality you talk about, this extensive awareness in which the particular is a detail? Is it some mysterious, mystical experience? If so then we are lost completely. Or is *this* perhaps what you are saying, that there is a whole field of existence, of which anger is a part, and that to be concerned with the part is to block out the extensive perception? But what is this extensive perception? I can only see the whole through all its particulars. And what whole do you mean? Are you talking about the whole of the mind, or the whole of existence, or the whole of myself, or the whole of life? What whole do you mean, and how can I see it?

Krishnamurti: The whole field of life: the mind, love, everything which is in life.

Questioner: How can I possibly see all that! I can understand that everything I see is partial, and that all my awareness is awareness of the particular, and that this strengthens the particular.

Krishnamurti: Let's put it this way: do you perceive with your mind and your heart separately, or do you see, hear, feel, think, all together, not fragmentarily?

Questioner: I don't know what you mean.

Krishnamurti: You hear a word, your mind tells you it is an insult, your feelings tell you you don't like it, your mind again intervenes to control or justify, and so on. Once again feeling takes over where the mind has concluded. In this way an event unleashes a chain-reaction of different parts of your being. What you hear has been broken up, made fragmentary, and if you concentrate on one of those fragments, you miss the total process of that hearing. Hearing can be fragmentary or it can be done with all your being, totally. So, by perception of the whole we mean perception with your eyes, your ears, your heart, your mind; not perception with each separately. It is giving your complete attention. In that attention, the particular, such as anger, has a different meaning since it is inter-related to many other issues.

Questioner: So when you say seeing the whole, you mean seeing with the whole of your being; it is a question of quality not quantity. Is that correct?

Krishnamurti: Yes, precisely. But *do* you see totally in this way or are you merely verbalising it? Do you see anger with your heart,

mind, ears and eyes? Or do you see anger as something un-
related to the rest of you, and therefore of great importance?
When you give importance to the whole you do not forget the
particular.

Questioner: But what happens to the particular, to anger?

Krishnamurti: You are aware of anger with your whole being. If
you are, is there anger? Inattention is anger, not attention. So
attention with your entire being is seeing the whole, and inattention is seeing the particular. To be aware of the whole, and
of the particular, and of the relationship between the two, is the
whole problem. We divide the particular from the rest and try
to solve it. And so conflict increases and there is no way out.

Questioner: When you speak then of seeing only the particular,
as anger, do you mean looking at it with only one part of your
being?

Krishnamurti: When you look at the particular with a fragment
of your being, the division between that particular and the fragment which is looking at it grows, and so conflict increases.
When there is no division there is no conflict.

Questioner: Are you saying that there is no division between this
anger and me when I look at it with all my being?

Krishnamurti: Exactly. Is this what you actually are doing, or are
you merely following the words? What is actually taking place?
This is far more important than your question.

Questioner: You ask me what is taking place. I am simply trying
to understand you.

Krishnamurti: Are you trying to understand me or are you seeing
the truth of what we are talking about, which is independent of
me? If you actually see the truth of what we are talking about,
then you are your own guru and your own disciple, which is to
understand yourself. This understanding cannot be learnt from
another.

MORALITY

Questioner: What is it to be virtuous? What makes one act right-eously? What is the foundation of morality? How do I know virtue without struggling for it? Is it an end in itself?

Krishnamurti: Can we discard the morality of society which is really quite immoral? Its morality has become respectable, approved by religious sanctions; and the morality of counter-revolution also soon becomes as immoral and respectable as that of well-established society. This morality is to go to war, to kill, to be aggressive, to seek power, to give hate its place; it is all the cruelty and injustice of established authority. This is not moral. But can one actually say that it is not moral? Because we are part of this society, whether we are conscious of it or not. Social morality is our morality, and can we easily put it aside? The ease with which we put it aside is the sign of our morality —not the effort it costs us to put it aside, not the reward, not the punishment for this effort but the consummate ease with which we discard it. If our behaviour is directed by the environment in which we live, controlled and shaped by it, then it is mechanical and heavily conditioned. And if our behaviour is the outcome of our own conditioned response, is it moral? If your action is based on fear and reward, is it righteous? If you behave rightly according to some ideological concept or principle, can that action be regarded as virtuous? So we must begin to find out how deeply we have discarded the morality of authority, imitation, conformity and obedience. Isn't fear the basis of our morality? Unless these questions are fundamentally answered for oneself, one cannot know what it is to be truly virtuous. As we said, with what ease you come out of this hypocrisy is of the greatest importance. If you merely disregard it, it doesn't indicate that you are moral: you might be merely psychopathic. If you live a life of routine and contentment, that is not morality either. The morality of the saint who conforms and follows the well-established tradition of sainthood is obviously not morality. So one can see that any conformity to a pattern, whether or not it is sanctioned by tradition, is not righteous behaviour. Only out of freedom can come virtue.

Can one free oneself with great skill from this network of what is considered moral? Skill in action comes with freedom, and so virtue.

Questioner: Can I free myself from social morality without fear, with the intelligence which is skill? I'm frightened at the very idea of being considered immoral by society. The young can do it, but I am middle-aged, and I have a family, and in my very blood there is respectability, the essence of the bourgeois. It is there, and I am frightened.

Krishnamurti: Either you accept social morality or reject it. You can't have it both ways. You can't have one foot in hell and the other in heaven.

Questioner: So what am I to do? I see now what morality is, and yet I'm being immoral all the time. The older I grow the more hypocritical I become. I despise the social morality, and yet I want its benefits, its comfort, its security, psychological and material, and the elegance of a good address. That is my actual, deplorable state. What am I to do?

Krishnamurti: You can't do anything but carry on as you are. It is much better to drop trying to be moral, stop trying to be concerned with virtue.

Questioner: But I can't, I want the other! I see the beauty and the vigour of it, the cleanliness of it. What I am holding on to is dirty and ugly, but I can't let it go.

Krishnamurti: Then there is no issue. You can't have virtue and respectability. Virtue is freedom. Freedom is not an idea, a concept. When there is freedom there is attention, and only in this attention can goodness flower.

SUICIDE

Questioner: I would like to talk about suicide—not because of any crisis in my own life, nor because I have any reason for suicide, but because the subject is bound to come up when one sees the tragedy of old age—the tragedy of physical disintegration, the breaking up of the body, and the loss of real life in people when this happens. Is there any reason to prolong life when one reaches that state, to go on with the remnants of it? Would it not perhaps be an act of intelligence to recognise when the usefulness of life is over?

Krishnamurti: If it was intelligence that prompted you to end life, that very intelligence would have forbidden your body to deteriorate prematurely.

Questioner: But is there not a moment when even the intelligence of the mind cannot prevent this deterioration? Eventually the body wears out—how does one recognise that time when it comes?

Krishnamurti: We ought to go into this rather deeply. There are several things involved in it, aren't there? The deterioration of the body, of the organism, the senility of the mind, and the utter incapacity that breeds resistance. We abuse the body endlessly through custom, taste and negligence. Taste dictates—and the pleasure of it controls and shapes the activity of the organism. When this takes place, the natural intelligence of the body is destroyed. In magazines one sees an extraordinary variety of food, beautifully coloured, appealing to your pleasures of taste,

50

not to what is beneficial for the body. So from youth onwards
you gradually deaden and destroy the instrument which should
be highly sensitive, active, functioning like a perfect machine.
That is part of it, and then there is the mind which for twenty,
thirty or eighty years has lived in constant battle and resistance.
It knows only contradiction and conflict—emotional or intellectual. Every form of conflict is not only a distortion but brings
with it destruction. These then are some of the basic inner and
outer factors of deterioration—the perpetually self-centred activity with its isolating processes.

Naturally there is the physical wearing out of the body as well
as the unnatural wearing out. The body loses its capacities and
memories, and senility gradually takes over. You ask, should
not such a person commit suicide, take a pill that will put him
out? Who is asking the question—the senile, or those who are
watching the senility with sorrow, with despair and fear of their
own deterioration?

Questioner: Well, obviously the question from my point of view
is motivated by distress at seeing senility in other people, for
it has not presumably set in myself yet. But isn't there also
some action of intelligence which sees ahead into a possible
breakdown of the body and asks the question whether it is not
simply a waste to go on once the organism is no longer capable
of intelligent life?

Krishnamurti: Will the doctors allow euthanasia, will the doctors
or the government permit the patient to commit suicide?

Questioner: That surely is a legal, sociological or, in some people's minds, a moral question, but that isn't what we are discussing here, is it? Aren't we asking whether the individual has the
right to end his own life, not whether society will permit it?

Krishnamurti: You are asking whether one has the right to take
one's own life—not only when one is senile or has become
aware of the approach of senility, but whether it is morally right
to commit suicide at any time?

Questioner: I hesitate to bring morality into it because that is a conditioned thing. I was attempting to ask the question on a straight issue of intelligence. Fortunately at the moment the issue does not confront me personally so I am able to look at it, I think, fairly dispassionately; but as an exercise in human intelligence, what is the answer?

Krishnamurti: You are saying, can an intelligent man commit suicide? Is that it?

Questioner: Or, can suicide be the action of an intelligent man, given certain circumstances?

Krishnamurti: It is the same thing. Suicide comes, after all, either from complete despair, brought about through deep frustration, or from insoluble fear, or from the awareness of the meaninglessness of a certain way of living.

Questioner: May I interrupt to say that this is generally so, but I am trying to ask the question outside any motivation. When one arrives at the point of despair then there is a tremendous motive involved and it is hard to separate the emotion from the intelligence; I am trying to stay within the realm of pure intelligence, without emotion.

Krishnamurti: You are saying, does intelligence allow any form of suicide? Obviously not.

Questioner: Why not?

Krishnamurti: Really one has to understand this word intelligence. Is it intelligence to allow the body to deteriorate through custom, through indulgence, through the cultivation of taste, pleasure and so on? Is that intelligence, is that the action of intelligence?

Questioner: No; but if one has arrived at a point in life where there may have been a certain amount of unintelligent use of the body which has not yet had any effect on it, one can't go back and re-live one's life.

Krishnamurti: Therefore, become aware of the destructive nature of the way we live and put an end to it immediately, not at some future date. The act of immediacy in front of danger is an act of sanity, of intelligence; and the postponement as well as the pursuit of pleasure indicate lack of intelligence.

Questioner: I see that.

Krishnamurti: But don't you also see something quite factual and true, that this isolating process of thought with its self-centred activity is a form of suicide? Isolation is suicide, whether it is the isolation of a nation or of a religious organisation, of a family or of a community. You are already caught in that trap which will ultimately lead to suicide.

Questioner: Do you mean the individual or the group?

Krishnamurti: The individual as well as the group. You are already caught in the pattern.

Questioner: Which will ultimately lead to suicide? But everybody doesn't commit suicide!

Krishnamurti: Quite right, but the element of the desire to escape is already there—to escape from facing facts, from facing "what is", and this escape is a form of suicide.

Questioner: This, I think, is the crux of what I am trying to ask, because it would seem from what you have just said that suicide is an escape. Obviously it is, ninety-nine times out of a hundred, but can there not also be—and this is my question—can there not also be a suicide that is not an escape, that is not an avoidance of what you call the "what is", but is on the contrary a response of intelligence to "what is"? One can say that many kinds of neurosis are forms of suicide; what I am trying to ask is whether suicide can ever be other than a neurotic response? Cannot it also be the response of facing a fact, of human intelligence acting on an untenable human condition?

Krishnamurti: When you use the words "intelligence" and "untenable condition" it is a contradiction. The two are in contradiction.

Questioner: You have said that if one is facing a precipice, or a deadly snake about to strike, intelligence dictates a certain action, which is an action of avoidance.

Krishnamurti: Is it an action of avoidance or an act of intelligence?

Questioner: Can they not be the same sometimes? If a car comes at me on the highway and I avoid it. . . .

Krishnamurti: That is an act of intelligence.

Questioner: But it is also an act of avoiding the car.

Krishnamurti: But that is the act of intelligence.

Questioner: Exactly. Therefore, is there not a corollary in living when the thing confronting you is insoluble and deadly?

Krishnamurti: Then you leave it, as you leave the precipice: step away from it.

Questioner: In that case the stepping away implies suicide.

Krishnamurti: No, the suicide is an act of unintelligence.

Questioner: Why?

Krishnamurti: I am showing it to you.

Questioner: Are you saying that an act of suicide is categorically, inevitably, a neurotic response to life?

Krishnamurti: Obviously. It is an act of unintelligence; it is an act which obviously means you have come to a point where you are so completely isolated that you don't see any way out.

Questioner: But I am trying for the purpose of this discussion to assume that there is no way out of the predicament, that one is not acting out of the motive of avoidance of suffering, that it is not stepping aside from reality.

Krishnamurti: Is there in life an occurrence, a relationship, an incident from which you cannot step aside?

Questioner: Of course, there are many.

Krishnamurti: Many? But why do you insist that suicide is the only way out?

Questioner: If one has a deadly disease there is no escaping it.

Krishnamurti: Be careful now, be careful of what we are saying. If I have cancer, and it is going to finish me, and the doctor says, "Well, my friend, you have got to live with it", what am I to do —commit suicide?

Questioner: Possibly.

Krishnamurti: We are discussing this theoretically. If I personally had terminal cancer, then I would decide, I would consider what to do. It wouldn't be a theoretical question. I would then find out what was the most intelligent thing to do.

Questioner: Are you saying that I may not ask this question theoretically, but only if I am actually in that position?

Krishnamurti: That is right. Then you will act according to your conditioning, according to your intelligence, according to your way of life. If your way of life has been avoidance and escape, a neurotic business, then obviously you take a neurotic attitude and action. But if you have led a life of real intelligence, in the total meaning of that word, then that intelligence will operate when there is terminal cancer. Then I may put up with it; then I may say that I will live the few more months or years left to me.

Questioner: Or you may not say that.

Krishnamurti: Or I may not say that; but don't let us say that suicide is inevitable.

Questioner: I never said that; I asked if under certain stringent circumstances, such as terminal cancer, suicide could possibly be an intelligent response to the situation.

Krishnamurti: You see, there is something extraordinary in this; life has brought you great happiness, life has brought you extraordinary beauty, life has brought you great benefits, and you went with it all. Equally, when you were unhappy you went with it, which is part of intelligence: now you come to terminal cancer and you say, "I cannot bear it any longer, I must put an end to life." Why don't you move with it, live with it, find out about it as you go along?

Questioner: In other words, there is no reply to this question until you are in the situation.

Krishnamurti: Obviously. But you see that is why it is very important, I feel, that we should face the fact, face "what is", from moment to moment, not theorise about it. If someone is ill, desperately ill with cancer, or has become completely senile—what is the most intelligent thing to do, not for a mere observer like me, but for the doctor, the wife or the daughter?

Questioner: One cannot really answer that, because it is a problem for another human being.

Krishnamurti: That's just it, that is just what I am saying.

Questioner: And one hasn't the right, it would seem to me, to decide about the life or death of another human being.

Krishnamurti: But we do. All the tyrannies do. And tradition does; tradition says you must live this way, you mustn't live that way.

Questioner: And it is also becoming a tradition to keep people alive beyond the point where nature would have given in. Through medical skill people are kept alive—well, it's hard to define what is a natural condition—but it seems most unnatural to survive for as long as many people do today. But that is a different question.

Krishnamurti: Yes, an entirely different question. The real question is, will intelligence allow suicide—even though doctors have said one has an incurable disease? One cannot possibly tell another what to do in this matter. It is for the human being who has the incurable disease to act according to his intelligence. If he is at all intelligent—which means that he has lived a life in which there has been love, care, sensitivity and gentleness—then such a person, at the moment when it arises, will act according to the intelligence which has operated in the past.

Questioner: Then this whole conversation is in a way meaningless because that is what would have happened anyway—because people would inevitably act according to what has happened in the past. They will either blow their brains out or sit and suffer until they die, or something in between.

Krishnamurti: No, it hasn't been meaningless. Listen to this; we have discovered several things—primarily that to live with intelligence is the most important thing. To live a way of life which is supremely intelligent demands an extraordinary alertness of mind and body, and we've destroyed the alertness of the body by unnatural ways of living. We are also destroying the mind, the brain, through conflict, through constant repression, constant explosion and violence. So if one lives a way of life that is a negation of all this, then that life, that intelligence, when confronted with incurable disease will act in the moment rightly.

Questioner: I see that I have asked you a question about suicide and have been given an answer on how to live rightly.

Krishnamurti: It is the only way. A man jumping over the bridge doesn't ask, "Shall I commit suicide?" He is doing it; it is finished. Whereas we, sitting in a safe house or in a laboratory, asking whether a man should or should not commit suicide, has no meaning.

Questioner: So it is a question one cannot ask.

Krishnamurti: No, it must be asked—whether one should or should not commit suicide. It must be asked, but find out what is behind the question, what is prompting the questioner, what is making him want to commit suicide. We know a man who has not committed suicide, although he is always threatening to do so, because he is completely lazy. He doesn't want to do a thing, he wants everybody to support him; such a man has already committed suicide. The man who is obstinate, suspicious, greedy for power and position, has also inwardly committed suicide. He lives behind a wall of images. So any man who lives with an image of himself, of his environment, his ecology, his political power or religion, is already finished.

Questioner: It would seem to me that what you are saying is that any life that is not lived directly. . . .

Krishnamurti: Directly and intelligently.

Questioner: Outside the shadows of images, of conditioning, of thinking. . . . Unless one lives that way, one's life is a kind of low-key existence.

Krishnamurti: Of course it is. Look at most people; they are living behind a wall—the wall of their knowledge, their desires, their ambitious drives. They are already in a state of neurosis and that neurosis gives them a certain security, which is the security of suicide.

Questioner: The security of suicide!

Krishnamurti: Like a singer, for example; to him the voice is the greatest security, and when that fails he is ready to commit suicide. What is really exciting and true is to find out for oneself a way of life that is highly sensitive and supremely intelligent; and this is not possible if there is fear, anxiety, greed, envy, the building of images or the living in religious isolation. That isolation is what all religions have supplied: the believer is definitely on the threshold of suicide. Because he has put all his faith in a belief, when that belief is questioned he is afraid and is ready to take on another belief, another image, commit another religious suicide. So, can a man live without any image, without any pattern, without any time-sense? I don't mean living in such a way as not to care what happens tomorrow or what happened yesterday. That is not living. There are those who say, "Take the present and make the best of it"; that is also an act of despair. Really one should not ask whether or not it is right to commit suicide; one should ask what brings about the state of mind that has no hope—though hope is the wrong word because hope implies a future; one should ask rather, how does a life come about that is without time? To live without time is really to have this sense of great love, because love is not of time, love is not something that was or will be; to explore this and live with it is the real question. Whether to commit suicide or not is the question of a man who is already partially dead. Hope is the most dreadful thing. Wasn't it Dante who said, "Leave hope behind when you enter the Inferno"? To him, paradise was hope; that's horrible.

Questioner: Yes, hope is its own inferno.

DISCIPLINE

Questioner: I've been brought up in a very restricted environment, in strict discipline, not only as to outward behaviour but also I was taught to discipline myself, to control my thoughts and appetites and to do certain things regularly. The result is that I find myself so hedged about that I can't do anything easily, freely and happily. When I see what is going on around me in this permissive society—the sloppiness, the dirt, the casual behaviour, the indifference to manners—I'm shocked, although at the same time I secretly desire to do some of these things myself. Discipline imposed certain values though; it brought with it frustrations and distortions, but surely some discipline is necessary—for instance, to sit decently, to eat properly, to speak with care? Without discipline one can't perceive the beauties of music or literature or painting. Good manners and training reveal a great many nuances in daily social commerce. When I observe the modern generation they have the beauty of youth, but without discipline it will soon fade away and they will become rather tiresome old men and women. There is a tragedy in all this. You see a young man, supple, eager, beautiful with clear eyes and a lovely smile, and a few years later you see him again and he is almost unrecognisable—sloppy, callous, indifferent, full of platitudes, highly respectable, hard, ugly, closed and sentimental. Surely discipline would have saved him. I, who have been disciplined almost out of existence, often wonder where the middle way is between this permissive society and the culture in which I was brought up. Isn't there a way to live without the distortion and suppression of discipline, and yet to be highly disciplined within oneself?

Krishnamurti: Discipline means to learn, not to conform, not to suppress, not to imitate the pattern of what accepted authority considers noble. This is a very complex question for in it are involved several things: to learn, to be austere, to be free, to be sensitive, and to see the beauty of love.

In learning there is no accumulation. Knowledge is different from learning. Knowledge is accumulation, conclusions, formulas, but learning is a constant movement, a movement without a centre, without a beginning or an end. To learn about oneself there must be no accumulation in one's learning: if there is, it is not learning about oneself but merely adding to one's accumulated knowledge of oneself. Learning is the freedom of perception, of seeing. And you cannot learn if you are not free. So this very learning is its own discipline—you don't have to discipline yourself and then learn. Therefore discipline is freedom. This denies all conformity and control, for control is the imitation of a pattern. A pattern is suppression, suppression of "what is", and the learning about "what is" is denied when there is a formula of what is good and what is bad. The learning about "what is" is the freedom from "what is". So learning is the highest form of discipline. Learning demands intelligence and sensitivity.

The austerity of the priest and the monk is harsh. They deny certain of their appetites but not others which custom has condoned. The saint is the triumph of harsh violence. Austerity is generally identified with self-denial through the brutality of discipline, drill and conformity. The saint is trying to break a record like the athlete. To see the falseness of this brings about its own austerity. The saint is stupid and shoddy. To see this is intelligence. Such intelligence will not go off the deep end to the opposite extreme. Intelligence is the sensitivity which understands, and therefore avoids, the extremes. But it is not the prudent mediocrity of remaining half-way between the two. To perceive all this clearly is to learn about it. To learn about it there must be freedom from all conclusions and bias. Such conclusions and bias are observation from a centre, the self, which wills and directs.

Questioner: Aren't you simply saying that to look properly you must be objective?

Krishnamurti: Yes, but the word objective is not enough. What we are talking about is not the harsh objectiveness of the microscope, but a state in which there is compassion, sensitivity and depth. Discipline, as we said, is learning, and learning about austerity does not bring about violence to oneself or to another. Discipline, as it is generally understood, is the act of will, which is violence.

People throughout the world seem to think that freedom is the fruit of prolonged discipline. To see clearly is its own discipline. To see clearly there must be freedom, not a controlled vision. So freedom is not at the end of discipline, but the understanding of freedom is its own discipline. The two go together inseparably: when you separate them there is conflict. To overcome that conflict, the action of will comes into being and breeds more conflict. This is an endless chain. So freedom is at the beginning and not at the end: the beginning is the end. To learn about all this is its own discipline. Learning itself demands sensitivity. If you are not sensitive to yourself—to your environment, to your relationships—if you are not sensitive to what is happening around you, in the kitchen or in the world, then however much you discipline yourself you only become more and more insensitive, more and more self-centred —and this breeds innumerable problems. To learn is to be sensitive to yourself and to the world outside you, for the world outside is you. If you are sensitive to yourself you are bound to be sensitive to the world. This sensitivity is the highest form of intelligence. It is not the sensitivity of a specialist—the doctor, the scientist or the artist. Such fragmentation does not bring sensitivity.

How can one love if there is no sensitivity? Sentimentality and emotionalism deny sensitivity because they are terribly cruel; they are responsible for wars. So discipline is not the drill of the sergeant—whether in the parade-ground or in yourself—which is the will. Learning all day long, and during sleep, has its own extraordinary discipline which is as gentle as the new spring leaf and as swift as the light. In this there is love. Love has its own discipline, and the beauty of it escapes a mind that is drilled, shaped, controlled, tortured. Without such a discipline the mind cannot go very far.

WHAT IS

Questioner: I have read a great deal of philosophy, psychology, religion and politics, all of which to a greater or lesser degree are concerned with human relationships. I have also read your books which all deal with thought and ideas, and somehow I'm fed up with it all. I have swum in an ocean of words, and wherever I go there are more words—and actions derived from those words are offered to me: advice, exhortations, promises, theories, analyses, remedies. Of course one sets all these aside —you yourself have really done so; but for most of those who have read you, or heard you, what you say is just words. There may be people for whom all this is more than words, for whom it is utterly real, but I'm talking about the rest of us. I'd like to go beyond the word, beyond the idea, and live in total relationship to all things. For after all, that is life. You have said that one has to be a teacher and a pupil to oneself. Can I live in the greatest simplicity, without principles, beliefs and ideals? Can I live freely, knowing that I am enslaved by the world? Crises don't knock on the door before they appear: challenges of everyday life are there before you are aware of them. Knowing all this, having been involved in many of these things, chasing various phantoms, I ask myself how I can live rightly and with love, clarity and effortless joy. I'm not asking *how* to live, but to *live*: the how denies the actual living itself. The nobility of life is not *practising* nobility.

Krishnamurti: After stating all this, where are you? Do you really want to live with benediction, with love? If you do, then where is the problem?

Questioner: I do want to, but that doesn't get me anywhere. I've wanted to live that way for years, but I can't.

Krishnamurti: So though you deny the ideal, the belief, the directive, you are very subtly and deviously asking the same thing which everybody asks: this is the conflict between the "what is" and the "what should be".

Questioner: Even without the "what should be", I see that the "what is" is hideous. To deceive myself into not seeing it would be much worse still.

Krishnamurti: If you see "what is" then you see the universe, and denying "what is" is the origin of conflict. The beauty of the universe is in the "what is"; and to live with "what is" without effort is virtue.

Questioner: The "what is" also includes confusion, violence, every form of human aberration. To live with that is what you call virtue. But isn't it callousness and insanity? Perfection doesn't consist simply in dropping all ideals! Life itself demands that I live it beautifully, like the eagle in the sky: to live the miracle of life with anything less than total beauty is unacceptable.

Krishnamurti: Then live it!

Questioner: I can't, and I don't.

Krishnamurti: If you can't, then live in confusion; don't battle with it. Knowing the whole misery of it, live with it: that is "what is". And to live with it without conflict frees us from it.

Questioner: Are you saying that our only fault is to be self-critical?

Krishnamurti: Not at all. You are not sufficiently critical. You go only so far in your self-criticism. The very entity that criticises must be criticised, must be examined. If the examination is comparative, examination by yardstick, then that yardstick is the ideal. If there is no yardstick at all—in other words, if there is no mind that is always comparing and measuring—you can observe the "what is", and then the "what is" is no longer the same.

Questioner: I observe myself without a yardstick, and I'm still ugly.

Krishnamurti: All examination means there is a yardstick. But is it possible to observe so that there is only observation, seeing, and nothing else—so that there is only perception without a perceiver?

Questioner: What do you mean?

Krishnamurti: There is looking. The assessment of the looking is interference, distortion in the looking: that is not looking; instead it is evaluation of looking—the two are as different as chalk and cheese. Is there a perception of yourself *without* distortion, only an absolute perception of yourself as you are?

Questioner: Yes.

Krishnamurti: In that perception is there ugliness?

Questioner: There is no ugliness in the perception, only in what is perceived.

Krishnamurti: The way you perceive is what you are. Righteousness is in purely looking, which is attention without the distortion of measure and idea. You came to enquire how to live beautifully, with love. To look without distortion is love, and the action of that perception is the action of virtue. That clarity of perception will act all the time in living. That is living like the eagle in the sky; that is living beauty and living love.

THE SEEKER

Questioner: What is it I'm seeking? I really don't know, but there is a tremendous longing in me for something much more than comfort, pleasure and the satisfaction of fulfilment. I happen to have had all these things, but this is something much more—something at an unfathomable depth that is crying to be released, trying to tell me something. I've had this feeling for many years but when I examine it I don't seem to be able to touch it. Yet it is always there, this longing to go beyond the mountains and the skies to find something. But perhaps this thing is there right in front of me, only I don't see it. Don't tell me how to look: I've read many of your writings and I know what you mean. I want to reach out my hand and take this thing very simply, knowing very well that I cannot hold the wind in my fist. It is said that if you operate on a tumour neatly you can pluck it out in one pocket, intact. In the same way I should like to take this whole earth, the heavens and the skies and the seas in one movement, and come upon that blessedness on the instant. Is this at all possible? How am I to cross to the other shore without taking a boat and rowing across the waters? I feel that's the only way.

Krishnamurti: Yes, that's the only way—to find oneself strangely and unaccountably on the other shore, and from there to live, act and do everything that one does in daily life.

Questioner: Is it only for the few? Is it for me? I really don't know what to do. I've sat silent; I've studied, examined, disciplined myself, rather intelligently I think, and of course I've long ago discarded the temples, the shrines and the priests. I refuse to go from one system to another; it is all too futile. So you see I have come here with complete simplicity.

Krishnamurti: I wonder if you really are so simple as you think! From what depth are you asking this question, and with what love and beauty? Can your mind and heart receive this? Are they sensitive to the slightest whisper of something that comes unexpectedly?

Questioner: If it is as subtle as all that, how true is it, and how real? Intimations of such subtlety are usually fleeting and unimportant.

Krishnamurti: Are they? Must everything be written out on the blackboard? Please, Sir, let us find out whether our minds and hearts are really capable of receiving immensity, and not just the word.

Questioner: I really don't know, that's my problem. I've done almost everything fairly intelligently, putting aside all the obvious stupidities of nationality, organised religion, belief—this endless passage of nothings. I think I have compassion, and I think my mind can grasp the subleties of life, but that surely is not enough? So what is needed? What have I to do or not to do?

Krishnamurti: Doing nothing is far more important than doing something. Can the mind be completely inactive, and thereby be supremely active? Love is not the activity of thought; it is not the action of good behaviour or social righteousness. As you cannot cultivate it, you can do nothing about love.

Questioner: I understand what you mean when you say that inaction is the highest form of action—which doesn't mean to do nothing. But somehow I cannot grasp it with my heart. Is it perhaps only because my heart is empty, tired of all action, that inaction seems to have an appeal? No. I comeback to my original feeling that there is this thing of love, and I know, too, that it is the only thing. But my hand is still empty after I have said that.

Krishnamurti: Does this mean that you are no longer seeking, no longer saying to yourself secretly, "I must reach, attain, there is something beyond the furthest hills"?

Questioner: You mean I must give up this feeling I have had for so long that there is something beyond all the hills?

Krishnamurti: It is not a question of giving up anything, but, as we said just now, there are only these two things: love, and the mind that is empty of thought. If you really have finished, if you really have shut the door on all the stupidities which man in his search for something has put together, if you really have finished with all these, then, are these things—love and the empty mind—just two more words, no different from any other ideas?

Questioner: I have a deep feeling that they are not, but I am not sure. So again I ask what I am to do.

Krishnamurti: Do you know what it means to commune with what we have just said about love and the mind?

Questioner: Yes, I think so.

Krishnamurti: I wonder if you do. If there is communion with these two things then there is nothing more to be said. If there is communion with these two things then all action will be from there.

Questioner: The trouble is that I still think there is something to be discovered which will put everything else in its right place, in its right order.

Krishnamurti: Without these two things there is no possibility of going further. And there may be no going anywhere at all!

Questioner: Can I be in communion with it all the time? I can see that when we are together I can be somewhat in communion with it. But can I maintain it?

Krishnamurti: To desire to maintain it is the noise, and therefore the losing of it.

ORGANISATION

Questioner: I have belonged to many organisations, religious, business and political. Obviously we must have some kind of organisation; without it life couldn't continue, so I've been wondering, after listening to you, what relationship there is between freedom and organization. Where does freedom begin and organization end? What is the relationship between religious organizations and Moksha or liberation?

Krishnamurti: As human beings living in a very complex society, organisations are needed to communicate, to travel, to bring food, clothes and shelter, for all the business of living together whether in cities or in the country. Now this must be organised efficiently and humanely, not only for the benefit of the few but for everyone, without the divisions of nationality, race or class. This earth is ours, not yours or mine. To live happily, physically, there must be sane, rational, efficient organisations. Now there is disorder because there is division. Millions go hungry while there is vast prosperity. There are wars, conflicts and every form of brutality. Then there is the organisation of belief—the organisation of religions, which again breeds disunity and war. The morality which man has pursued has led to this disorder and chaos. This is the actual state of the world. And when you ask what is the relationship between organisation and freedom, are you not separating freedom from everyday existence? When you separate it in this way as being something entirely different from life, isn't this, in itself, conflict and disorder? So really the question is: is it possible to live in freedom and to organise life from this freedom?

Questioner: Then there would be no problem. But the organisation of life isn't made by yourself; others make it for you—the government and others send you to war or determine your job. So you cannot simply organise for yourself out of freedom. The whole point of my question is that the organisation imposed on us by the government, by society, by morality, is not freedom. And if we reject it we find ourselves in the midst of a revolution, or some sociological reformation, which is a way of starting the same old cycle all over again. Inwardly and outwardly we are born into organisation, which limits freedom. We either submit or revolt. We are caught in this trap. So there seems to be no question of organising anything out of freedom.

Krishnamurti: We do not realise that we have created society, this disorder, these walls; each one of us is responsible for it all. What we are, society is. Society is not different from us. If we are in conflict, avaricious, envious, fearful, we bring about such a society.

Questioner: There is a difference between the individual and society. I am a vegetarian; society slaughters animals. I don't want to go to war; society will force me to do so. Are you telling me that this war is my doing?

Krishnamurti: Yes, it's your responsibility. You have brought it about by your nationality, your greed, envy and hate. You are responsible for war as long as you have those things in your heart, as long as you belong to any nationality, creed or race. It is only those who are free of those things who can say that they have not created this society. Therefore our responsibility is to see that we change, and to help others to change, without violence and bloodshed.

Questioner: That means organised religion.

Krishnamurti: Certainly not. Organised religion is based on belief and authority.

Questioner: Where does this get us in our original question regarding the relationship between freedom and organisation? Organisation is always imposed or inherited from the environment, and freedom is always from the inside, and these two clash.

Krishnamurti: Where are you going to start? You must start from freedom. Where there is freedom there is love. This freedom and love will show you when to co-operate and when not to co-operate. This is not an act of choice, because choice is the result of confusion. Love and freedom are intelligence. So what we are concerned with is not the division between organisation and freedom but whether we can live in this world without division at all. It is division which denies freedom and love, not organisation. When organisation divides, it leads to war. Belief in any form, ideals, however noble or effective, breed division. Organised religion is the cause of division, just like nationality and power-groups. So be concerned with those things which divide, those things which bring about division between man and man, whether they be individual or collective. The family, the church, and the State bring about such division. What is important is the movement of thought which divides. Thought itself is always divisive, so all action based on an idea or an ideology is divisive. Thought cultivates prejudice, opinion, judgement. Man in himself, being divided, seeks freedom out of this division. Not being able to find it he hopes to integrate the various divisions, and of course this is not possible. You cannot integrate two prejudices. To live in this world in freedom means to live with love, eschewing every form of division. When there is freedom and love, then this intelligence will act in co-operation, and will also know when not to co-operate.

LOVE AND SEX

Questioner: I'm a married man with several children. I've lived rather a dissipated life in search of pleasure, but a fairly civilised life too, and I've made a success of it financially. But now I'm middle-aged and am feeling concerned, not only about my family but also about the way the world is going. I'm not given to brutality or violent feelings, and I have always considered that forgiveness and compassion are the most important things in life. Without these man becomes sub-human. So if I may I should like to ask you what love is. Is there really such a thing? Compassion must be part of it, but I always feel that love is something much vaster, and if we could explore it together perhaps I should then make my life into something worthwhile before it is too late. I have really come to ask this one thing—what is love?

Krishnamurti: Before we begin to go into this we must be very clear that the word is not the thing, the description is not the described, because any amount of explanation, however subtle and clever, will not open the heart to the immensity of love. This we must understand, and not merely stick to words; words are useful for communication, but in talking about something that is really non-verbal we must establish a communion between us, so that both of us feel and realise the same thing at the same time, with a fullness of mind and heart. Otherwise we will be playing with words. How can one approach this really very subtle thing that cannot be touched by the mind? We must go rather hesitatingly. Shall we first see what love is not, and then perhaps we may be able to see what it is? Through negation we may come upon the positive, but merely to pursue the positive leads to assumptions and conclusions which bring about division. You are asking what love is. We are saying we may come upon it when we know what it is not. Anything that brings about a division, a separation, is not love, for in that there is conflict, strife and brutality.

Questioner: What do you mean by a division, a separation that brings about strife—what do you mean by it?

Krishnamurti: Thought in its very nature is divisive. It is thought that cultivates desire.

Questioner: Will you go into desire a bit more?

Krishnamurti: There is the seeing of a house, the sensation that it is lovely, then there is the desire to own it and to have pleasure from owning it, then there is the effort to get it. All this constitutes the centre, and this centre is the cause of division. This centre is the feeling of a "me", which is the cause of division, because this very feeling of "me" is the feeling of separation. People have called this the ego, and all kinds of other names— the "lower self" as opposed to some idea of a "higher self"— but there is no need to be complicated about it; it is very simple. Where there is the centre, which is the feeling of "me", which in its activities isolates itself, there is division and resistance. And all this is the process of thought. So when you ask what is love, it is not of this centre. Love is not pleasure and pain, nor hate nor violence in any form.

Questioner: Therefore in this love you speak of there can be no sex because there cannot be desire?

Krishnamurti: Don't, please, come to any conclusion. We are investigating, exploring. Any conclusion or assumption prevents further enquiry. To answer this question we have also to look at the energy of thought. Thought, as we have said, sustains pleasure by thinking about something that has been pleasurable, cultivating the image, the picture. Thought engenders pleasure. Thinking about the sexual act become lust, which is entirely different from the act of sex. What most people are concerned with is the passion of lust. Craving before and after sex is lust. This craving is thought. Thought is not love.

Questioner: Can there be sex without this desire of thought?

Krishnamurti: You have to find out for yourself. Sex plays an extraordinarily important part in our lives because it is perhaps the only deep, first-hand experience we have. Intellectually and emotionally we conform, imitate, follow, obey. There is pain and strife in all our relationships, except in the act of sex. This act, being so different and beautiful, we become addicted to, so it in turn becomes a bondage. The bondage is the demand for its continuation—again the action of the centre which is divisive. One is so hedged about—intellectually, in the family, in the community, through social morality, through religious sanctions—so hedged about that there is only this one relationship left in which there is freedom and intensity. Therefore we give tremendous importance to it. But if there were freedom all around then this would not be such a problem. We make it a problem because we can't get enough of it, or because we feel guilty at having got it, or because in getting it we break the rules which society has laid down. It is the old society which calls the new society permissive because for the new society sex is a part of life. In freeing the mind from the bondage of imitation, authority, conformity and religious prescriptions, sex has its own place, but it won't be all-consuming. From this one can see that freedom is essential for love—not the freedom of revolt, not the freedom of doing what one likes nor of indulging openly or secretly one's cravings, but rather the freedom which comes in the understanding of this whole structure and nature of the centre. Then freedom is love.

Questioner: So freedom is not licence?

Krishnamurti: No. Licence is bondage. Love is not hate, nor jealousy, nor ambition, nor the competitive spirit with its fear of failure. It is not the love of god nor the love of man—which again is a division. Love is not of the one or of the many. When there is love it is personal and impersonal, with and without an object. It is like the perfume of a flower; one or many can smell it: what matters is the perfume, not to whom it belongs.

Questioner: Where does forgiveness come in all this?

Krishnamurti: When there is love there can be no forgiveness. Forgiveness comes only after you have accumulated rancour; forgiveness is resentment. Where there is no wound there is no need for healing. It is inattention that breeds resentment and hate, and you become aware of them and then forgive. Forgiveness encourages division. When you are conscious that you are forgiving, then you are sinning. When you are conscious that you are tolerant, then you are intolerant. When you are conscious that you are silent, then there is no silence. When you deliberately set about to love, then you are violent. As long as there is an observer who says, "I am" or "I am not", love cannot be.

Questioner: What place has fear in love?

Krishnamurti: How can you ask such a question? Where one is, the other is not. When there is love you can do what you will.

PERCEPTION

Questioner: You use different words for perception. You sometimes say "perception", but also "observe", "see", "understand", "be aware of". I suppose you use all these words to
mean the same thing: to see clearly, completely, wholly. Can one
see anything totally? We're not talking of physical or technical
things, but psychologically can you perceive or understand anything totally? Isn't there always something concealed so that
you see only partially? I'd be most obliged if you could go into
this matter rather extensively. I feel this is an important question because it may perhaps be the clue to a great many things
in life. If I could understand myself totally then perhaps I would
have all my problems solved and be a happy super-human being. When I talk about it I feel rather excited at the possibility
of going beyond my little world with its problems and agonies.
So what do you mean by perceiving, seeing? *Can* one see oneself completely?

Krishnamurti: We always look at things partially. Firstly because
we are inattentive and secondly because we look at things from
prejudices, from verbal and psychological images about what
we see. So we never see anything completely. Even to look
objectively at nature is quite arduous. To look at a flower without any image, without any botanical knowledge—just to observe it—becomes quite difficult because our mind is
wandering, uninterested. And even if it is interested it looks at
the flower with certain appreciations and verbal descriptions
which seem to give the observer a feeling that he has really

looked at it. Deliberate looking is not looking. So we really never look at the flower. We look at it through the image. Perhaps it is fairly easy to look at something that doesn't deeply touch us, as when we go to the cinema and see something which stirs us for the moment but which we soon forget. But to observe ourselves without the image—which is the past, our accumulated experience and knowledge—happens very rarely. We have an image about ourselves. We think we ought to be this and not that. We have built a previous idea about ourselves and through it we look at ourselves. We think we are noble or ignoble, and seeing what we actually are either depresses us or frightens us. So we cannot look at ourselves; and when we do, it is partial observation; and anything that is partial or incomplete doesn't bring understanding. It is only when we can look at ourselves totally that there is a possibility of being free from what we observe. Our perception is not only with the eyes, with the senses, but also with the mind, and obviously the mind is heavily conditioned. So intellectual perception is only partial perception, yet perceiving with the intellect seems to satisfy most of us, and we think we understand. A fragmentary understanding is the most dangerous and destructive thing. And that is exactly what is happening all over the world. The politician, the priest, the business man, the technician; even the artist—all of them see only partially. And therefore they are really very destructive people. As they play a great part in the world their partial perception becomes the accepted norm, and man is caught in this. Each of us is at the same time the priest, the politician, the business man, the artist, and many other fragmentary entities. And each of us is also the battlefield of all these conflicting opinions and judgements.

Questioner: I see this clearly. I'm using the word see intellectually, of course.

Krishnamurti: If you see this totally, not intellectually or verbally or emotionally, then you will act and live quite a different kind of life. When you see a dangerous precipice or are faced by a dangerous animal there is no partial understanding or partial action; there is complete action.

Questioner: But we are not faced with such dangerous crises every moment of our lives.

Krishnamurti: We *are* faced with such dangerous crises all the time. You have become accustomed to them, or are indifferent to them, or you leave it to others to solve the problems; and these others are equally blind and lopsided.

Questioner: But how am I to be aware of these crises all the time, and why do you say there is a crisis all the time?

Krishnamurti: The whole of life is in each moment. Each moment is a challenge. To meet this challenge inadequately is a crisis in living. We don't want to see that these are crises, and we shut our eyes to escape from them. So we become blinder, and the crises augment.

Questioner: But how am I to perceive totally? I'm beginning to understand that I see only partially, and also to understand the importance of looking at myself and the world with complete perception, but there is so much going on in me that it is difficult to decide what to look at. My mind is like a great cage full of restless monkeys.

Krishnamurti: If you see one movement totally, in that totality every other movement is included. If you understand one problem completely, then you understand all human problems, for they are all inter-related. So the question is: can one understand, or perceive, or see, one problem so completely that in the very understanding of it one has understood the rest? This problem must be seen while it is happening, not after or before, as memory or as an example. For instance, it is no good now for us to go into anger or fear; the thing to do is to observe them as they arise. Perception is instantaneous: you understand something instantly or not at all: seeing, hearing, understanding are instantaneous. Listening and looking have duration.

Questioner: My problem goes on. It exists in a span of time. You are saying that seeing is instantaneous and therefore out of time. What gives jealousy or any other habit, or any other problem, duration?

Krishnamurti: Don't they go on because you have not looked at them with sensitivity, choiceless awareness, intelligence? You have looked partially and therefore allowed them to continue. And in addition, wanting to get rid of them is another problem with duration. The incapacity to deal with something makes of it a problem with duration, and gives it life.

Questioner: But how am I to see the whole thing instantly? How am I to understand so that it never comes back?

Krishnamurti: Are you laying emphasis on never or on understanding? If you lay emphasis on never it means you want to escape from it permanently, and this means the creation of a second problem. So we have only one question, which is how to see the problem so completely that one is free of it. Perception can only be out of silence, not out of a chattering mind. The chattering may be the wanting to get rid of it, reduce it, escape from it, suppress it or find a substitute for it, but it is only a quiet mind that sees.

Questioner: How am I to have a quiet mind?

Krishnamurti: You don't see the truth that only a quiet mind sees. How to get a quiet mind doesn't arise. It is the truth that the mind must be quiet, and seeing the truth of this frees the mind from chattering. Perception, which is intelligence, is then operating, not the assumption that you must be silent in order to see. Assumption can also operate but that is a partial, fragmentary operation. There is no relationship between the partial and the total; the partial cannot grow into the total. Therefore seeing is of the greatest importance. Seeing is attention, and it is only inattention that gives rise to a problem.

Questioner: How can I be attentive all the time? It's impossible!

Krishnamurti: That's quite right, it *is* impossible. But to be aware of your inattention is of the greatest importance, not how to be attentive all the time. It is greed that asks the question, "How can I be attentive all the time?" One gets lost in the practice of being attentive. The practice of being attentive is inattention. You cannot practise to be beautiful, or to love. When hate ceases the other is. Hate can cease only when you give your whole attention to it, when you learn and do not accumulate knowledge about it. Begin very simply.

Questioner: What is the point of your talking if there is nothing we can practise after having heard you?

Krishnamurti: The hearing is of the greatest importance, not what you practise afterwards. The hearing is the instantaneous action. The practice gives duration to problems. Practice is total inattention. Never practise: you can only practise mistakes. Learning is always new.

SUFFERING

Questioner: I seem to have suffered a great deal all my life, not physically, but through death and loneliness and the utter futility of my existence. I had a son whom I greatly loved. He died in an accident. My wife left me, and that caused a great deal of pain. I suppose I am like thousands of other middle-class people with sufficient money and a steady job. I'm not complaining of my circumstances but I want to understand what sorrow means, why it comes at all. One has been told that wisdom comes through sorrow, but I have found quite the contrary.

Krishnamurti: I wonder what you have learnt from suffering? Have you learnt anything at all? What has sorrow taught you?

Questioner: It has certainly taught me never to be attached to people, and a certain bitterness, a certain aloofness, and not to allow my feeling to run away with me. It has taught me to be very careful not to get hurt again.

Krishnamurti: So, as you say, it hasn't taught you wisdom; on the contrary it has made you more cunning, more insensitive. Does sorrow teach one anything at all except the obvious self-protective reactions?

Questioner: I have always accepted suffering as part of my life, but I feel now, somehow, that I'd like to be free of it, free of all the tawdry bitterness and indifference without again going through all the pain of attachment. My life is so pointless and empty, utterly self-enclosed and insignificant. It's a life of mediocrity, and perhaps that mediocrity is the greatest sorrow of all.

Krishnamurti: There is the personal sorrow and the sorrow of the world. There is the sorrow of ignorance and the sorrow of time. This ignorance is the lack of knowing oneself, and the sorrow of time is the deception that time can cure, heal and change. Most people are caught in that deception and either worship sorrow or explain it away. But in either case it continues, and one never asks oneself if it can come to an end.

Questioner: But I am asking now if it can come to an end, and how? How am I to end it? I understand that it's no good running away from it, or resisting it with bitterness and cynicism. What am I to do to end the grief which I have carried for so long?

Krishnamurti: Self-pity is one of the elements of sorrow. Another element is being attached to someone and encouraging or fostering his attachment to you. Sorrow is not only there when attachment fails you but its seed is in the very beginning of that attachment. In all this the trouble is the utter lack of knowing oneself. Knowing oneself is the ending of sorrow. We are afraid to know ourselves because we have divided ourselves into the good and the bad, the evil and the noble, the pure and the impure. The good is always judgeing the bad, and these fragments are at war with each other. This war is sorrow. To end sorrow is to see the fact and not invent its opposite, for the opposites contain each other. Walking in this corridor of opposites is sorrow. This fragmentation of life into the high and the low, the noble and the ignoble, God and the Devil, breeds conflict and pain. When there is sorrow, there is no love. Love and sorrow cannot live together.

Questioner: Ah! But love can inflict sorrow on another. I may love another and yet bring him sorrow.

Krishnamurti: Do you bring it, if you love, or does he? If another is attached to you, with or without encouragement, and you turn away from him and he suffers, is it you or he who has brought about his suffering?

Questioner: You mean I am not responsible for someone else's sorrow, even if it is on my account? How does sorrow ever end then?

Krishnamurti: As we have said, it is only in knowing oneself completely that sorrow ends. Do you know yourself at a glance, or hope to after a long analysis? Through analysis you cannot know yourself. You can only know yourself without accumulation, in relationship, from moment to moment. This means that one must be aware, without any choice, of what is actually taking place. It means to see oneself as one is, without the opposite, the ideal, without the knowledge of what one has been. If you look at yourself with the eyes of resentment or rancour then what you see is coloured by the past. The shedding of the past all the time when you see yourself is the freedom from the past. Sorrow ends only when there is the light of understanding, and this light is not lit by one experience or by one flash of understanding; this understanding is lighting itself all the time. Nobody can give it to you—no book, trick, teacher or saviour. The understanding of yourself is the ending of sorrow.

THE HEART AND THE MIND

Questioner: Why is it that man has divided his being into different compartments—the intellect and the emotions? Each seems to exist independently of the other. These two driving forces in life are often so contradictory that they seem to tear apart the very fabric of our being. To bring them together so that man can act as a total entity has always been one of the principal aims of life. And added to these two things within man there is a third which is his changing environment. So these two contradictory things within him are further in opposition to the third which appears to be outside himself. Here is a problem so confusing, so contradictory, so vast that the intellect invents an outside agency called God to bring them together, and this further complicates the whole business. There is only this one problem in life.

Krishnamurti: You seem to be carried away by your own words. Is this really a problem to you or are you inventing it in order to have a good discussion? If it is for a discussion then it has no real content. But if it is a real problem then we can go into it deeply. Here we have a very complex situation, the inner dividing itself into compartments and further separating itself from its environment. And still further, it separates the environment, which it calls society, into classes, races and economic, national and geographic groups. This seems to be what is actually going on in the world and we call it living. Being unable to solve this problem we invent a super-entity, an agency which we hope will bring about a harmony and a binding quality in ourselves and between us. This binding quality which we call religion brings about another factor of division in its turn. So the question becomes: what will bring about a complete harmony of living in which there are no divisions but a state in which the intellect and the heart are both the expression of a total entity? That entity is not a fragment.

Questioner: I agree with you, but how is this to be brought about? This is what man has always longed for and has sought through all religions and all political and social utopias.

Krishnamurti: You ask how. The "how" is the great mistake. It is the separating factor. There is your "how" and my "how" and somebody else's "how". So if we never used that word we would be really enquiring and not seeking a method to achieve a determined result. So can you put away altogether this ideas of a recipe, a result? If you can define a result you already know it and therefore it is conditioned and not free. If we put away the recipe then we are both capable of enquiring if it is at all possible to bring about a harmonious whole without inventing an outside agency, for all outside agencies, whether they are environmental or super-environmental, only increase the problem.

First of all, it is the mind that divides itself as feeling, intellect and environment; it is the mind that invents the outside agency; it is the mind that creates the problem.

Questioner: This division is not only in the mind. It is even stronger in the feelings. The Muslims and Hindus do not think themselves separate, they *feel* themselves separate, and it is this feeling that actually makes them separate and makes them destroy each other.

Krishnamurti: Exactly: the thinking and the feeling are one; they have been one from the beginning and that is exactly what we are saying. So our problem is not the integration of the different fragments but the understanding of this mind and heart which are one. Our problem is not how to get rid of classes or

how to build better utopias or breed better political leaders or
new religious teachers. Our problem is the mind. To come to
this point not theoretically but to see it actually is the highest
form of intelligence. For then you do not belong to any class or
religious group; then you are not a Muslim, a Hindu, a Jew or
a Christian. So we now have only one issue: Why does the mind
of man divide? It not only divides its own functions into feelings
and thoughts but separates itself as the "I" from the "you", and
the "we" from the "they". The mind and the heart are one.
Don't let us forget it. Remember it when we use the word
"mind". So our problem is, why does the mind divide?

Questioner: Yes.

Krishnamurti: The mind is thought. All the activity of thought is
separation, fragmentation. Thought is the response of memory
which is the brain. The brain must respond when it sees a
danger. This is intelligence, but this same brain has somehow
been conditioned not to see the danger of division. Its actions
are valid and necessary when they deal with facts. Equally, it will
act when it sees the fact that division and fragmentation are
dangerous to it. This is not an idea or an ideology or a principle
or a concept—all of which are idiotic and separative: it is a fact.
To see danger the brain has to be very alert and awake, all of
it, not just a segment of it.

Questioner: How is it possible to keep the whole brain awake?

Krishnamurti: As we said, there is no "how" but only seeing the
danger, that is the whole point. The seeing is not the result of
propaganda or conditioning; the seeing is with the whole brain.
When the brain is completely awake then the mind becomes
quiet. When the brain is completely awake there is no fragmentation, no separation, no duality. The quality of this quietness
is of the highest importance. You can make the mind quiet by
drugs and all kinds of tricks but such deceptions breed various
other forms of illusion and contradiction. This quietness is the
highest form of intelligence which is never personal or imper-

sonal, never yours or mine. Being anonymous, it is whole and immaculate. It defies description for it has no quality. This is awareness, this is attention, this is love, this is the highest. The brain must be completely awake, that's all. As the man in the jungle must keep terribly awake to survive, so the man in the jungle of the world must keep terribly awake to live completely.

BEAUTY AND THE ARTIST

Questioner: I wonder what an artist is? There on the banks of the Ganges, in a dark little room, a man sits weaving a most beautiful saree in silk and gold, and in Paris in his atelier another man is painting a picture which he hopes will bring him fame. Somewhere there is a writer cunningly spinning out stories stating the old, old problem of man and woman; then there is the scientist in his laboratory and the technician putting together a million parts so that a rocket may go to the moon. And in India a musician is living a life of great austerity in order to transmit faithfully the distilled beauty of his music. There is the housewife preparing a meal, and the poet walking alone in the woods. Aren't these all artists in their own way? I feel that beauty is in the hands of everybody, but they don't know it. The man who makes beautiful clothes or excellent shoes, the woman who arranged those flowers on your table, all of them seem to work with beauty. I often wonder why it is that the painter, the sculptor, the composer, the writer—the so-called creative artists—have such extraordinary importance in this world and not the shoemaker or the cook. Aren't they creative too? When you consider all the varieties of expression which people consider beautiful, then what place has a true artist in life, and who is the true artist? It is said that beauty is the very essence of all life. Is that building over there, which is considered to be so beautiful, the expression of that essence? I should greatly appreciate it if you would go into this whole question of beauty and the artist.

Krishnamurti: Surely the artist is one who is skilled in action? This action is in life and not outside of life. Therefore it is living skillfully that truly makes an artist. This skill can operate for a few hours in the day when he is playing an instrument, writing poems or painting pictures, or it can operate a bit more if he is skilled in many such fragments—like those great men of the Renaissance who worked in several different media. But the few hours of music or writing may contradict the rest of his living which is in disorder and confusion. So is such a man an artist at all? The man who plays the violin with artistry and keeps his eye on his fame isn't interested in the violin, he is only exploiting it to be famous, the "me" is far more important than the music, and so it is with the writer or the painter with an eye on fame. The musician identifies his "me" with what he considers to be beautiful music, and the religious man identifies his "me" with what he considers to be the sublime. All these are skilled in their particular little fields but the rest of the vast field of life is disregarded. So we have to find out what is skill in action, in living, not only in painting or in writing or in technology, but how one can live the whole of life with skill and beauty. Are skill and beauty the same? Can a human being—whether he be an artist or not—live the whole of his life with skill and beauty? Living is action and when that action breeds sorrow it ceases to be skillful. So can a man live without sorrow, without friction, without jealousy and greed, without conflict of any kind? The issue is not who is an artist and who is not an artist but whether a human being, you or another, can live without torture and distortion. Of course it is profane to belittle great music, great sculpture, great poetry or dancing, or to sneer at it; that is to be unskilled in one's own life. But the artistry and beauty which is skill in action should operate throughout the day, not just during a few hours of the day. This is the real challenge, not just playing the piano beautifully. You must play it beautifully if you touch it at all, but that is not enough. It is like cultivating a small corner of a huge field. We are concerned with the whole field and that field is life. What we always do is to neglect the whole field and concentrate on fragments, our own or other people's. Artistry is to be completely awake and therefore to be skillful in action in the whole of life, and this is beauty.

Questioner: What about the factory worker or office employee? Is he an artist? Doesn't his work preclude skill in action and so deaden him that he has no skill in anything else either? Is he not conditioned by his work?

Kirshnamurti: Of course he is. But if he wakes up he will either leave his work or so transform it that it becomes artistry. What is important is not the work but the waking up to the work. What is important is not the conditioning of the work but to wake up.

Questioner: What do you mean, wake up?

Krishnamurti: Are you awakened only by circumstances, by challenges, by some disaster or joy? Or is there a state of being awake without any cause? If you are awakened by an event, a cause, then you depend on it, and when you depend on something—whether it be a drug, sex, painting or music—you are allowing yourself to be put to sleep. So any dependence is the end of skill, the end of artistry.

Questioner: What is this other awakened state that has no cause? You are talking about a state in which there is neither a cause nor an effect. Can there be a state of mind that is not the result of some cause? I don't understand that because surely everything we think and everything we are is the result of a cause? There is this endless chain of cause and effect.

Krishnamurti: This chain of cause and effect is endless because the effect becomes the cause and the cause begets further effects, and so on.

Questioner: Then what action is there outside this chain? .

Krishnamurti: All we know is action with a cause, a motive, action which is a result. All action is in relationship. If relationship is based on cause it is cunning adaptation, and therefore inevitably leads to another form of dullness. Love is the only thing that is causeless, that is free; it is beauty, it is skill, it is art. Without love there is no art. When the artist is playing beautifully there is no "me"; there is love and beauty, and this is art. This is skill in action. Skill in action is the absence of the "me". Art is the absence of the "me". But when you neglect the whole field of life and concentrate on only a little part—however much the "me" may then be absent, you are still living unskillfully and therefore you are not an artist of life. The absence of "me" in living is love and beauty, which brings its own skill. This is the greatest art: living skillfully in the whole field of life.

Questioner: Oh Lord! How am I to do that? I see it and feel it in my heart but how can I maintain it?

Krishnamurti: There is no way to maintain it, there is no way to nourish it, there is no practising of it; there is only the seeing of it. Seeing is the greatest of all skills.

DEPENDENCE

Questioner: I should like to understand the nature of dependence. I have found myself depending on so many things—on women, on different kinds of amusement, on good wine, on my wife and children, on my friends, on what people say. Fortunately I no longer depend on religious entertainment, but I depend on the books I read to stimulate me and on good conversation. I see that the young are also dependent, perhaps not so much as I am, but they have their own particular forms of dependence. I have been to the East and have seen how there they depend on the guru and the family. Tradition there has greater importance and is more deeply rooted than it is in Europe, and, of course, very much more so than in America. But we all seem to depend on something to sustain us, not only physically but, much more, inwardly. So I am wondering whether it is at all possible to be really free of dependence, and should one be free of it?

Krishnamurti: I take it you are concerned with the psychological inward attachments. The more one is attached the greater the dependence. The attachment is not only to persons but to ideas and to things. One is attached to a particular environment, to a particular country and so on. And from this springs dependence and therefore resistance.

Questioner: Why resistance?

Krishnamurti: The object of my attachment is my territorial or my sexual domain. This I protect, resisting any form of encroachment on it from others. I also limit the freedom of the person to whom I am attached and limit my own freedom. So attachment is resistance. I am attached to something or somebody. That attachment is possessiveness; possessiveness is resistance, so attachment is resistance.

Questioner: Yes, I see that.

Krishnamurti: Any form of encroachment on my possessions leads to violence, legally or psychologically. So attachment is violence, resistance, imprisonment—the imprisonment of oneself and of the object of attachment. Attachment means this is mine and not yours, keep off! So this relationship is resistance against others. The whole world is divided into mine and yours: my opinion, my judgement, my advice, my God, my country— an infinity of such nonsense. Seeing all this taking place, not in abstraction but actually in our daily life, we can ask why there is this attachment to people, things and ideas. Why does one depend? All being is relationship and all relationship is in this dependence with its violence, resistance and domination. We have made the whole world into this. Where one possesses one must dominate. We meet beauty, love springs up, and immediately it turns to attachment and all this misery begins and the love has gone out of the window. Then we ask, "What has happened to our great love?" This is actually what is happening in our daily life. And, seeing all this, we can now ask: why is man invariably attached, not only to that which is lovely, but also to every form of illusion and to so many idiotic fancies?

Freedom is not a state of non-dependence; it is a positive state in which there isn't any dependence. But it is not a result, it has no cause. This must be understood very clearly before we can go into the question of why man depends or falls into the trap of attachment with all its miseries. Being attached we try to cultivate a state of independence—which is another form of resistance.

Questioner: So what is freedom? You say it is not the negation of dependence or the ending of dependence; you say it is not freedom from something, but just freedom. So what is it? Is it an abstraction or an actuality?

Krishnamurti: It is not an abstraction. It is the state of mind in which there is no form of resistance whatsoever. It is not like a river accommodating itself to boulders here and there, going round or over them. In this freedom there are no boulders at all, only the movement of the water.

Questioner: But the boulder of attachment is there, in this river of life. You can't just speak about another river in which there are no boulders.

Krishnamurti: We are not avoiding the boulder or saying it doesn't exist. We must first understand freedom. It is not the same river as the one in which there are the boulders.

Questioner: I have still got my river with its boulders, and that's what I came to ask about, not about some other unknown river without boulders. That's no good to me.

Krishnamurti: Quite right. But you must understand what freedom is in order to understand your boulders. But don't let us flog this simile to death. We must consider both freedom and attachment.

Questioner: What has my attachment to do with freedom or freedom with my attachment?

Krishnamurti: In your attachment there is pain. You want to be rid of this pain, so you cultivate detachment which is another form of resistance. In the opposite there is no freedom. These two opposites are identical and mutually strengthen each other. What you are concerned with is how to have the pleasures of attachment without its miseries. You cannot. That is why it is important to understand that freedom does not lie in detachment. In the process of understanding attachment there is freedom, not in running away from attachment. So our question now is, why are human beings attached, dependent?

Being nothing, being a desert in oneself, one hopes through another to find water. Being empty, poor, wretched, insufficient, devoid of interest or importance, one hopes through another to be enriched. Through the love of another one hopes to forget oneself. Through the beauty of another one hopes to acquire beauty. Through the family, through the nation, through the lover, through some fantastic belief, one hopes to cover this desert with flowers. And God is the ultimate lover. So one puts hooks into all these things. In this there is pain and uncertainty, and the desert seems more arid than ever before. Of course it is neither more nor less arid; it is what it was, only one has avoided looking at it while escaping through some form of attachment with its pain, and then escaping from that pain into detachment. But one remains arid and empty as before. So instead of trying to escape, either through attachment or through detachment, can we not become aware of this fact, of this deep inward poverty and inadequacy, this dull, hollow isolation? That is the only thing that matters, not attachment or detachment. Can you look at it without any sense of condemnation or evaluation? When you do, are you looking at it as an observer who looks at the observed, or without the observer?

Questioner: What do you mean, the observer?

Krishnamurti: Are you looking at it from a centre with all its conclusions of like and dislike, opinion, judgement, the desire to be free of this emptiness and so on—are you looking at this aridness with the eyes of conclusion—or are you looking with eyes that are completely free? When you look at it with eyes that are free, there is no observer. If there is no observer, is there the thing observed as loneliness, emptiness and wretchedness?

Questioner: Do you mean to say that that tree doesn't exist if I look at it without conclusion, without a centre which is the observer?

Krishnamurti: Of course the tree exists.

Questioner: Why does loneliness disappear but not the tree when I look without the observer?

Krishnamurti: Because the tree is not created by the centre, by the mind of the "me". The mind of the "me" in all its self-centred activity has created this emptiness, this isolation, but when that mind, without the centre, looks, the self-centred activity ends. So the loneliness is not. Then the mind functions in freedom. Looking at the whole structure of attachment and detachment, and the movement of pain and pleasure, we see how the mind of the "me" builds its own desert and its own escapes. When the mind of the "me" is still, then there is no desert and there is no escape.

BELIEF

Questioner: I am one of those people who really believe in God. In India I followed one of the great modern saints who, because he believed in God, brought about great political changes there. In India the whole country throbs to the beat of God. I have heard you talk against belief so probably you don't believe in God. But you are a religious person and therefore there must be in you some kind of feeling of the Supreme. I have been all over India and through many parts of Europe, visiting monasteries, churches and mosques, and everywhere I have found this very strong, compelling belief in God whom one hopes shapes one's life. Now since you don't believe in God, although you are a religious person, what exactly is your position with regard to this question? Why don't you believe? Are you an atheist? As you know, in Hinduism you can be an atheist or a theist and yet be equally well a Hindu. Of course it's different with the Christians. If you don't believe in God you can't be a Christian. But that's beside the point. The point is that I have come to ask you to explain your position and demonstrate to me its validity. People follow you and therefore you have a responsibility, and therefore I am challenging you in this way.

Krishnamurti: Let us first of all clear up this last point. There are no followers, and I have no responsibility to you or to the people who listen to my talks. Also I am not a Hindu or anything else, for I don't belong to any group, religious or otherwise. Each one must be a light to himself. Therefore there is no teacher, no disciple. This must be clearly understood from the very beginning otherwise one is influenced, one becomes a slave to propaganda and persuasions. Therefore anything that is being said now is not dogma or creed or persuasion: we either meet together in understanding or we don't. Now, you said most emphatically that you believe in God and you probably want through that belief to experience what one might call the godhead. Belief involves many things. There is belief in facts that you may not have seen but can verify, like the existence of New York or the Eiffel Tower. Then you may believe that your wife is faithful though you don't actually know it. She might be unfaithful in thought yet you believe she is faithful because you don't actually see her going off with someone else; she may deceive you in daily thought, and you most certainly have done the same too. You believe in reincarnation, don't you, though there is no certainty that there is any such thing? However, that belief has no validity in your life, has it? All Christians believe that they must love but they do not love—like everyone else they go about killing, physically or psychologically. There are those who do not believe in God and yet do good. There are those who believe in God and kill for that belief; those who prepare for war because they claim they want peace, and so on. So one has to ask oneself what need there is to believe at all in anything, though this doesn't deny the extraordinary mystery of life. But belief is one thing and "what is" is another. Belief is a word, a thought, and this is not the thing, any more than your name is actually you.

Through experience you hope to touch the truth of your belief, to prove it to yourself, but this belief conditions your experience. It isn't that the experience comes to prove the belief, but rather that the belief begets the experience. Your belief in God will give you the experience of what you call God. You will always experience what you believe and nothing else. And this invalidates your experience. The Christian will see virgins, angels and Christ, and the Hindu will see similar deities in extravagant plurality. The Muslim, the Buddhist, the Jew and the Communist are the same. Belief conditions its own supposed proof. What is important is not what you believe but only why you believe at all. Why *do* you believe? And what difference does it make to what actually *is* whether you believe one thing or another? Facts are not influenced by belief or disbelief. So one has to ask why one believes at all in anything; what is the basis of belief? Is it fear, is it the uncertainly of life—the fear of the unknown, the lack of security in this ever-changing world? Is it the insecurity of relationship, or is it that faced with the immensity of life, and not understanding it, one encloses oneself in the refuge of belief? So, if I may ask you, if you had no fear at all, would you have any belief?

Questioner: I am not at all sure that I am afraid, but I love God, and it is this love that makes me believe in Him.

Krishnamurti: Do you mean to say you are devoid of fear? And therefore know what love is?

Questioner: I have replaced fear with love and so to me fear is non-existent, and therefore my belief is not based on fear.

Krishnamurti: Can you substitute love for fear? Is that not an act of thought which is afraid and therefore covers up the fear with the word called love, again a belief? You have covered up that fear with a word and you cling to the word, hoping to dissipate fear.

Questioner: What you are saying disturbs me greatly. I am not at all sure I want to go on with this, because my belief and my love have sustained me and helped me to lead a decent life. This questioning of my belief brings about a sense of disorder of which, quite frankly, I am afraid.

Krishnamurti: So there *is* fear, which you are beginning to discover for yourself. This disturbs you. Belief comes from fear and is the most destructive thing. One must be free of fear and of belief. Belief divides people, makes them hard, makes them hate each other and cultivate war. In a roundabout way, unwillingly, you are admitting that fear begets belief. Freedom from belief is necessary to face the fact of fear. Belief like any other ideal is an escape from "what is". When there is no fear then the mind is in quite a different dimension. Only then can you ask the question whether there is a God or not. A mind clouded by fear or belief is incapable of any kind of understanding, any realisation of what truth is. Such a mind lives in illusion and can obviously not come upon that which is Supreme. The Supreme has nothing to do with your or anybody else's belief, opinion or conclusion.

Not knowing, you believe, but to know is not to know. To know is within the tiny field of time, and the mind that says, "I know", is bound by time and so cannot possibly understand that which *is*. After all, when you say, "I know my wife and my friend", you know only the image or the memory, and this is the past. Therefore you can never actually know anybody or anything. You cannot know a living thing, only a dead thing. When you see this you will no longer think of relationship in terms of knowing. So one can never say, "There is no God", or "I know God". Both these are a blasphemy. To understand that which *is* there must be freedom, not only from the known but also from the fear of the known and from the fear of the unknown.

Questioner: You speak of understanding that which "is" and yet you deny the validity of knowing. What is this understanding if it is not knowing?

Krishnamurti: The two are quite different. Knowing is always related to the past and therefore it binds you to the past. Unlike knowing, understanding is not a conclusion, not accumulation. If you have listened you have understood. Understanding is attention. When you attend completely you understand. So the understanding of fear is the ending of fear. Your belief can therefore no longer be the predominant factor; the understanding of fear is predominant. When there is no fear there is freedom. It is only then that one can find what is true. When that which "is" is not distorted by fear then that which "is" is true. It is not the word. You cannot measure truth with words. Love is not a word nor a belief nor something that you can capture and say, "It is mine". Without love and beauty that which you call God is nothing at all.

DREAMS

Questioner: I have been told by professionals that dreaming is as vital as daytime thinking and activity, and that I would find my daily living under great stress and strain if I did not dream. They insist, and here I'm using not their jargon but my own words, that during certain periods of sleep the movement of the eyelids indicates refreshing dreams and that these bring a certain clarity to the brain. I am wondering whether the stillness of the mind which you have often spoken about might not bring greater harmony to living than the equilibrium brought about by patterns of dreams. I should also like to ask why the language of dreams is one of symbols.

Krishnamurti: Language itself is a symbol, and we are used to symbols: we see the tree through the image which is the symbol of the tree, we see our neighbour through the image we have about him. Apparently it is one of the most difficult things for a human being to look at anything directly, not through images, opinions, conclusions, which are all symbols. And so in dreams symbols play a large part; in this there is great deception and danger. The meaning of a dream is not always clear to us, although we realise it is in symbols and try to decipher them. When we see something, we speak of it so spontaneously that we do not recognise that words are also symbols. All this indicates, doesn't it, that there is direct communication in technical matters but seldom in human relationships and understanding? You don't need symbols when somebody hits you. That is a direct communication. This is a very interesting point: the mind refuses to see things directly, to be aware of itself without the word and the symbol. You say the sky is blue. The listener then deciphers this according to his own reference of blueness and transmits it to you in his own cipher. So we live in symbols, and dreams are a part of this symbolic process. We are incapable of direct and immediate perception without the symbols, the words, the prejudices and conclusions. The reason for this is also quite apparent: it is part of the self-centred activity with its defences, resistances, escapes and fears. There is a ciphered response in the activity of the brain, and dreams must naturally be symbolic because during the waking hours we are incapable of direct response or perception.

Questioner: It seems to me that this then is an inherent function of the brain.

Krishnamurti: Inherent means something permanent, inevitable and lasting. Surely any psychological state can be changed. Only the deep, constant demand of the brain for the physical security of the organism is inherent. Symbols are a device of the brain to protect the psyche; this is the whole process of thought. The "me" is a symbol, not an actuality. Having created the symbol of the "me", thought identifies itself with its conclusion, with the formula, and then defends it: all misery and sorrow come from this.

Questioner: Then how do I get around it?

Krishnamurti: When you ask how to get around it, you are still holding on to the symbol of the "me" which is fictitious; you become something separate from what you see, and so duality arises.

Questioner: May I come back another day to continue this?

* * *

Questioner: You were good enough to let me come back, and I should like to continue where we left off. We were talking about symbols in dreams and you pointed out that we live by symbols, deciphering them according to our gratification. We do this not only in dreams but in everyday life; it is our usual behaviour. Most of our actions are based on the interpretation of the symbols or images that we have. Strangely, after having talked with you the other day, my dreams have taken a peculiar turn. I have had very disturbing dreams and the interpretation of those dreams took place as they were happening within the dreams. It was a simultaneous process; the dream was being interpreted by the dreamer. This has never happened to me before.

Krishnamurti: During our waking hours, there is always the observer, different from the observed, the actor, separate from his action. In the same way there is the dreamer separate from his dream. He thinks it is separate from himself and therefore in need of interpretation. But is the dream separate from the dreamer, and is there any need to interpret it? When the observer is the observed what need is there to interpret, to judge, to evaluate? This need would exist only if the observer were different from the thing observed. This is very important to understand. We have separated the thing observed from the observer and from this arises not only the problem of interpretation but also conflict, and the many problems connected with it. This division is an illusion. This division between groups, races, nationalities, is fictitious. We are human beings, undivided by names, by labels. When the labels become all-important, division takes place, and then wars and all other struggles come into being.

Questioner: How then do I understand the content of the dream? It must have significance. Is it an accident that I dream of some particular event or person?

Krishnamurti: We should really look at this quite differently. Is there anything to understand? When the observer thinks he is different from the thing observed there is an attempt to understand that which is outside himself. The same process goes on within him. There is the observer wishing to understand the thing he observes, which is himself. But when the observer *is* the observed, there is no question of understanding; there is only observation. You say that there is something to understand in the dream, otherwise there would be no dream, you say that the dream is a hint of something unresolved that one should understand. You use the word "understand", and in that very word is the dualistic process. You think there is an "I", and a thing to be understood, whereas in reality these two entities are one and the same. Therefore your search for a meaning in the dream is the action of conflict.

Questioner: Would you say the dream is an expression of something in the mind?

Krishnamurti: Obviously it is.

Questioner: I do not understand how it is possible to regard a dream in the way you are describing it. If it has no significance, why does it exist?

Krishnamurti: The "I" is the dreamer, and the dreamer wants to see significance in the dream which he has invented or projected, so both are dreams, both are unreal. This unreality has become real to the dreamer, to the observer who thinks of himself as separate. The whole problem of dream interpretation arises out of this separation, this division between the actor and the action.

Questioner: I am getting more and more confused, so may we go over it again differently? I can see that a dream is the product of my mind and not separate from it, but dreams seem to come from levels of the mind which have not been explored, and so they seem to be intimations of something alive in the mind.

Krishnamurti: It is not your particular mind in which there are hidden things. Your mind is the mind of man; your consciousness is the whole of man. But when you particularise it as *your* mind, you limit its activity, and because of this limitation, dreams arise. During waking hours observe without the observer, who is the expression of limitation. Any division is a limitation. Having divided itself into a "me" and a "not me", the "me", the observer, the dreamer, has many problems—among them dreams and the interpretation of dreams. In any case, you will see the significance or the value of a dream only in a limited way because the observer is always limited. The dreamer perpetuates his own limitation, therefore the dream is always the expression of the incomplete, never of the whole.

Questioner: Pieces are brought back from the moon in order to understand the composition of the moon. In the same way we try to understand human thinking by bringing back pieces from our dreams, and examining what they express.

Krishnamurti: The expressions of the mind are the fragments of the mind. Each fragment expresses itself in its own way and contradicts other fragments. A dream may contradict another dream, one action another action, one desire another desire. The mind lives in this confusion. A part of the mind says it must understand another part, such as a dream, an action or a desire. So each fragment has its own observer, its own activity; then a super-observer tries to bring them all into harmony. The super-observer is also a fragment of the mind. It is these contradictions, these divisions, that breed dreams.

So the real question is not the interpretation or the understanding of a particular dream; it is the perception that these many fragments are contained in the whole. Then you see yourself as a whole and not as a fragment of a whole.

Questioner: Are you saying, Sir, that one should be aware during the day of the whole movement of life, not just one's family life, or business life, or any other individual aspect of life?

Krishnamurti: Consciousness is the whole of man and does not belong to a particular man. When there is the consciousness of one particular man there is the complex problem of fragmentation, contradiction and war. When there is awareness of the total movement of life in a human being during the waking hours, what need is there for dreams at all? This total awareness, this attention, puts an end to fragmentation and to division. When there is no conflict whatsoever the mind has no need for dreams.

Questioner: This certainly opens a door through which I see many things.

TRADITION

Questioner: Can one really be free of tradition? Can one be free of anything at all? Or is it a matter of side-stepping it and not being concerned with any of it? You talk a great deal about the past and its conditioning—but can I be really free of this whole background of my life? Or can I merely modify the background according to the various outward demands and challenges, adjust myself to it rather than become free of it? It seems to me that this is one of the most important things, and I'd like to understand it because I always feel that I am carrying a burden, the weight of the past. I would like to put it down and walk away from it, never come back to it. Is that possible?

Krishnamurti: Doesn't tradition mean carrying the past over to the present? The past is not only one's particular set of inheritances but also the weight of all the collective thought of a particular group of people who have lived in a particular culture and tradition. One carries the accumulated knowledge and experience of the race and the family. All this is the past—the carrying over from the known to the present—which shapes the future. Is not the teaching of all history a form of tradition? You are asking if one can be free of all this. First of all, why does one want to put down this burden? Why?

Questioner: I think it's fairly simple. I don't want to be the past —I want to be myself; I want to be cleansed of this whole tradition so that I can be a new human being. I think in most of us there is this feeling of wanting to be born anew.

Krishnamurti: You cannot possibly be the new just by wishing for it. Or by struggling to be new. You have not only to understand the past but also you have to find out who you are. Are you not the past? Are you not the continuation of what has been, modified by the present?

Questioner: My actions and my thoughts are, but my existence isn't.

Krishnamurti: Can you separate the two, action and thought, from existence? Are not thought, action, existence, living and relationship all one? This fragmentation into "me" and "not-me" is part of this tradition.

Questioner: Do you mean that when I am not thinking, when the past is not operating, I am obliterated, that I have ceased to exist?

Krishnamurti: Don't let us ask too many questions, but consider what we began with. Can one be free of the past—not only the recent but the immemorial, the collective, the racial, the human, the animal? You are all that, you are not separate from that. And you are asking whether you can put all that aside and be born anew. The "you" *is* that, and when you wish to be reborn as a new entity, the new entity you imagine is a projection of the old, covered over with the word "new". But underneath, you are the past. So the question is, can the past be put aside or does a modified form of tradition continue forever, changing, accumulating, discarding, but always the past in different combinations? The past is the cause and the present is the effect, and today, which is the effect of yesterday, becomes the cause of tomorrow. This chain is the way of thought, for thought is the past. You are asking whether one can stop this movement of yesterday into today. Can one look at the past to examine it, or is that not possible at all? To look at it the observer must be outside it—and he isn't. So here arises another issue. If the observer himself is the past then how can the past be isolated for observation?

Questioner: I can look at something objectively. . . .

Krishnamurti: But you, who are the observer, are the past trying to look at itself. You can objectify yourself only as an image which you have put together through the years in every form of relationship, and so the "you" which you objectify is memory and imagination, the past. You are trying to look at yourself as though you were a different entity from the one who is looking, but you *are* the past, with its old judgements, evaluations and so on. The action of the past is looking at the memory of the past. Therefore there is never relief from the past. The continuous examination of the past by the past perpetuates the past; this is the very action of the past, and this is the very essence of tradition.

Questioner: Then what action is possible? If I am the past—and I can see that I am—then whatever I do to chisel away the past is adding to it. So I am left helpless! What can I do? I can't pray because the invention of a god is again the action of the past. I can't look to another, for the other is also the creation of my despair. I can't run away from it all because at the end of it I am still there with my past because that image is my own projection too. Seeing all this, I am really left helpless, and in despair.

Krishnamurti: Why do you call it helplessness and despair? Aren't you translating what you see as the past into an emotional anxiety because you cannot achieve a certain result? In so doing you are again making the past act. Now, can you look at all this movement of the past, with all its traditions, without wanting to be free of it, change it, modify it or run away from it—simply observe it without any reaction?

Questioner: But as we have been saying all through this conversation, how can I observe the past if I am the past? I can't look at it at all!

Krishnamurti: Can you look at yourself, who are the past, without any movement of thought, which is the past? If you can look without thinking, evaluating, liking, disliking, judgeing, then there *is* a looking with eyes that are not touched by the past. It is to look in silence, without the noise of thought. In this silence there is neither the observer nor the thing which he is looking at as the past.

Questioner: Are you saying that when you look without evaluation or judgement the past has disappeared? But it hasn't—there are still the thousands of thoughts and actions and all the pettiness which were rampant only a moment ago. I look at them and they are still there. How can you say that the past has disappeared? It may momentarily have stopped acting. . . .

Krishnamurti: When the mind is silent that silence is a new dimension, and when there is any rampant pettiness it is instantly dissolved, because the mind has now a different quality of energy which is not the energy engendered by the past. This is what matters: to have that energy that dispels the carrying over of the past. The carrying over of the past is a different kind of energy. The silence wipes the other out; the greater absorbs the lesser and remains untouched. It is like the sea, receiving the dirty river and remaining pure. This is what matters. It is only this energy that can wipe away the past. Either there is silence or the noise of the past. In this silence the noise ceases and the new is this silence. It is not that *you* are made new. This silence is infinite and the past is limited. The conditioning of the past breaks down in the fullness of silence.

CONDITIONING

Questioner: You have talked a great deal about conditioning and have said that one must be free of this bondage, otherwise one remains imprisoned always. A statement of this kind seems so outrageous and unacceptable! Most of us are very deeply conditioned and we hear this statement and throw up our hands and run away from such extravagant expression, but I have taken you seriously—for, after all, you have more or less given your life to this kind of thing, not as a hobby but with deep seriousness—and therefore I should like to discuss it with you to see how far the human being can uncondition himself. Is it really possible, and if so, what does it mean? Is it possible for me having lived in a world of habits, traditions and the acceptance of orthodox notions in so many matters—is it possible for me really to throw off this deep-rooted conditioning? What exactly do you mean by conditioning, and what do you mean by freedom from conditioning?

Krishnamurti: Let us take the first question first. We are conditioned—physically, nervously, mentally—by the climate we live in and the food we eat, by the culture in which we live, by the whole of our social, religious and economic environment, by our experience, by education and by family pressures and influences. All these are the factors which condition us. Our conscious and unconscious responses to all the challenges of our environment— intellectual, emotional, outward and inward—all these are the action of conditioning. Language is conditioning; all thought is the action, the response of conditioning.

Knowing that we are conditioned we invent a divine agency which we piously hope will get us out of this mechanical state. We either postulate its existence outside or inside ourselves—as the atman, the soul, the Kingdom of Heaven which is within, and who knows what else! To these beliefs we cling desperately, not seeing that they themselves are part of the conditioning factor which they are supposed to destroy or redeem. So not being able to uncondition ourselves in this world, and not even seeing that conditioning is the problem, we think that freedom is in Heaven, in Moksha, in Nirvana. In the Christian myth of original sin and in the whole eastern doctrine of Samsara, one sees that the factor of conditioning has been felt, though rather obscurely. If it had been clearly seen, naturally these doctrines and myths would not have arisen. Nowadays the psychologists also try to get to grips with this problem, and in doing so condition us still further. Thus the religious specialists have conditioned us, the social order has conditioned us, the family which is part of it has conditioned us. All this is the past which makes up the open as well as the hidden layers of the mind. *En passant* it is-interesting to note that the so-called individual doesn't exist at all, for his mind draws on the common reservoir of conditioning which he shares with everybody else, so the division between the community and the individual is false: there is only conditioning. This conditioning is action in all relationships—to things, people and ideas.

Questioner: Then what am I to do to free myself from it all? To live in this mechanical state is not living at all, and yet all action, all will, all judgements are conditioned—so there is apparently nothing I can do about conditioning which isn't conditioned! I am tied hand and foot.

Krishnamurti: The very factor of conditioning in the past, in the present and in the future, is the "me" which thinks in terms of time, the "me" which exerts itself; and now it exerts itself in the demand to be free; so the root of all conditioning is the thought which is the "me". The "me" is the very essence of the past, the "me" is time, the "me" is sorrow—the "me" endeavours to free itself from itself, the "me" makes efforts, struggles to achieve, to deny, to become. This struggle to become is time in which there is confusion and the greed for the more and the better. The "me" seeks security and not finding it transfers the search to heaven; the very "me" that identifies itself with something greater in which it hopes to lose itself—whether that be the nation, the ideal or some god—is the factor of conditioning.

Questioner: You have taken everything away from me. What am I without this "me"?

Krishnamurti: If there is no "me" you are unconditioned, which means you are nothing.

Questioner: Can the "me" end without the effort of the "me"?

Krishnamurti: The effort to become something is the response, the action, of conditioning.

Questioner: How can the action of the "me" stop?

Krishnamurti: It can stop only if you see this whole thing, the whole business of it. If you see it in action, which is in relationship, the seeing is the ending of the "me". Not only is this seeing an action which is not conditioned but also it acts upon conditioning.

Questioner: Do you mean to say that the brain—which is the result of vast evolution with its infinite conditioning—can free itself?

Krishnamurti: The brain is the result of time; it is conditioned to protect itself physically, but when it tries to protect itself psychologically then the "me" begins, and all our misery starts. It is this effort to protect itself psychologically that is the affirmation of the "me". The brain can learn, can acquire knowledge technologically, but when it acquires knowledge psychologically then that knowledge asserts itself in relationship as the "me" with its experiences, its will and its violence. This is what brings division, conflict and sorrow to relationship.

Questioner: Can this brain be still and only operate when it has to work technologically—only operate when knowledge is demanded in action, as for example in learning a language, driving a car or building a house?

Krishnamurti: The danger in this is the dividing of the brain into the psychological and the technological. This again becomes a contradiction, a conditioning, a theory. The real question is whether the brain, the whole of it, can be still, quiet, and respond efficiently only when it has to in technology or in living. So we are not concerned with the psychological or the technological; we ask only, can this whole mind be completely still and function only when it has to? We say it can and this is the understanding of what meditation is.

* * *

Questioner: If I may I should like to continue where we left off yesterday. You may remember that I asked two questions: I asked what is conditioning and what is freedom from conditioning, and you said let us take the first question first. We hadn't time to go into the second question, so I should like to ask today, what is the state of the mind that is free from all its conditioning? After talking with you yesterday it became very clear to me how deeply and strongly I am conditioned, and I saw —at least I think I saw—an opening, a crack in this structure of conditioning. I talked the matter over with a friend and in taking certain factual instances of conditioning I saw very clearly how deeply and venomously one's actions are affected by it. As you said at the end, meditation is the emptying of the mind of all conditioning so that there is no distortion or illusion. How is one to be free of all distortion, all illusion? What is illusion?

Krishnamurti: It is so easy to deceive oneself, so easy to convince oneself of anything at all. The feeling that one must *be* something is the beginning of deception, and, of course, this idealistic attitude leads to various forms of hypocrisy. What makes illusion? Well, one of the factors is this constant comparison between what is and what should be, or what might be, this measurement between the good and the bad—thought trying to improve itself, the memory of pleasure, trying to get more pleasure, and so on. It is this desire for more, this dissatisfaction, which makes one accept or have faith in something, and this must inevitably lead to every form of deception and illusion. It is desire and fear, hope and despair, that project the goal, the conclusion to be experienced. Therefore this experience has no reality. All so-called religious experiences follow this pattern. The very desire for enlightenment must also breed the acceptance of authority, and this is the opposite of enlightenment. Desire, dissatisfaction, fear, pleasure, wanting more, wanting to change, all of which is measurement—this is the way of illusion.

Questioner: Do you really have no illusion at all about anything?

Krishnamurti: I am not all the time measuring myself or others. This freedom from measurement comes about when you are really living with what is—neither wishing to change it nor judgeing it in terms of good and bad. Living with something is not the acceptance of it: it is there whether you accept it or not. Living with something is not identifying yourself with it either.

Questioner: Can we go back to the question of what this freedom is that one really wants? This desire for freedom expresses itself in everybody, sometimes in the stupidest ways, but I think one can say that in the human heart is always this deep longing for freedom which is never realised; there is this incessant struggle to be free. I know I am not free; I am caught in so many wants. How am I to be free, and what does it mean to be really honestly free?

Krishnamurti: Perhaps this may help us to understand it: total negation is that freedom. To negate everything we consider to be positive, to negate the total social morality, to negate all inward acceptance of authority, to negate everything one has said or concluded about reality, to negate all tradition, all teaching, all knowledge except technological knowledge, to negate all experience, to negate all fulfilment, to negate all commitments to act in a particular way, to negate all ideas, all principles, all theories. Such negation is the most positive action, therefore it is freedom.

Questioner: If I chisel away at this, bit by bit, I shall go on forever and that itself will be my bondage. Can it all wither away in a flash, can I negate the whole human deception, all the values and aspirations and standards, *immediately*? Is it really possible? Doesn't it require enormous capacity, which I lack, enormous understanding, to see all this in a flash and leave it exposed to the light, to that intelligence you have talked about? I wonder, Sir, if you know what this entails. To ask me, an ordinary man with an ordinary education, to plunge into something which seems like an incredible nothingness. . . . Can I do it? I don't even know what it means to jump into it! It's like asking me to become all of a sudden the most beautiful, innocent, lovely human being. You see I am really frightened now, not the way I was frightened before. I am faced now with something which I know is true, and yet my utter incapacity to do it binds me. I see the beauty of this thing, to be really completely nothing, but. . .

Krishnamurti: You know, it is only when there is emptiness in oneself, not the emptiness of a shallow mind but the emptiness that comes with the total negation of everything one has been and should be and will be—it is only in this emptiness that there is creation; it is only in this emptiness that something new can take place. Fear is the thought of the unknown, so you are really frightened of leaving the known, the attachments, the satisfactions, the pleasurable memories, the continuity and security which give comfort. Thought is comparing this with what it thinks is emptiness. This imagination of emptiness is fear, so fear is thought. To come back to your question—can this mind negate everything it has known, the total content of its own conscious and unconscious self, which is the very essence of yourself ? Can you negate yourself completely? If not, there is no freedom. Freedom is not freedom from something—that is only a reaction; freedom comes in total denial.

Questioner: But what is the good of having such freedom? You are asking me to die, aren't you?

Krishnamurti: Of course! I wonder how you are using the word "good" when you say what is the good of this freedom? Good in terms of what? The known? Freedom is the absolute good and its action is the beauty of everyday life. In this freedom alone there is living, and without it how can there be love? Everything exists and has its being in this freedom. It is everywhere and nowhere. It has no frontiers. Can you die now to everything you know and not wait for tomorrow to die? This freedom is eternity and ecstasy and love.

HAPPINESS

Questioner: What is happiness? I have always tried to find it but
somehow it hasn't come my way. I see people enjoying themselves in so many different ways and many of the things they do
seem so immature and childish. I suppose they are happy in
their own way, but I want a different kind of happiness. I have
had rare intimations that it might be possible to get it, but
somehow it has always eluded me. I wonder what I can do to feel
really completely happy?

Krishnamurti: Do you think happiness is an end in itself? Or
does it come as a secondary thing in living intelligently?

Questioner: I think it is an end in itself because if there is happiness then whatever you do will be harmonious; then you will do
things effortlessly, easily, without any friction. I am sure that
whatever you do out of this happiness will be right.

Krishnamurti: But is this so? Is happiness an end in itself? Virtue
is not an end in itself. If it is, then it becomes a very small affair.
Can you seek happiness? If you do then probably you will find
an imitation of it in all sorts of distractions and indulgences.
This is pleasure. What is the relationship between pleasure and
happiness?

Questioner: I have never asked myself.

Krishnamurti: Pleasure which we pursue is mistakenly called
happiness, but can you pursue happiness, as you pursue pleasure? Surely we must be very clear as to whether pleasure is

happiness. Pleasure is gratification, indulgence, entertainment, stimulation. Most of us think pleasure is happiness, and the greatest pleasure we consider to be the greatest happiness. And is happiness the opposite of unhappiness? Are you trying to be happy because you are unhappy and dissatisfied? Has happiness got an opposite at all? Has love got an opposite? Is your question about happiness the result of being unhappy?

Questioner: I am unhappy like the rest of the world and naturally I don't want to be, and that is what is driving me to seek happiness.

Krishnamurti: So happiness to you is the opposite of unhappiness. If you were happy you wouldn't seek it. So what is important is not happiness but whether unhappiness can end. That is the real problem, isn't it? You are asking about happiness because you are unhappy and you ask this question without finding out whether happiness is the opposite of unhappiness.

Questioner: If you put it that way, I accept it. So my concern really is how to be free from the misery I am in.

Krishnamurti: Which is more important—to understand unhappiness or to pursue happiness? If you pursue happiness it becomes an escape from unhappiness and therefore it will always remain, covered over perhaps, hidden, but always there, festering inside. So what is your question now?

Questioner: My question now is why am I miserable? You have very neatly pointed out to me my real state, rather than given me the answer I want, so now I am faced with this question, how am I to get rid of the misery I am in?

Krishnamurti: Can an outside agency help you to get rid of your own misery, whether that outside agency be God, a master, a drug or a saviour? Or can one have the intelligence to understand the nature of unhappiness and deal with it immediately?

Questioner: I have come to you because I thought you might help me, so you could call yourself an outside agency. I want help and I don't care who gives it to me.

Krishnamurti: In accepting or giving help several things are involved. If you accept it blindly you will be caught in the trap of one authority or another, which brings with it various other problems, such as obedience and fear. So if you start off wanting help, not only do you not get help—because nobody can help you anyway—but in addition you get a whole series of new problems; you are deeper in the mire than ever before.

Questioner: I think I understand and accept that. I have never thought it out clearly before. How then can I develop the intelligence to deal with unhappiness on my own, and immediately? If I had this intelligence surely I wouldn't be here now, I wouldn't be asking you to help me. So my question now is, can I get this intelligence in order to solve the problem of unhappiness and thereby attain happiness?

Krishnamurti: You are saying that this intelligence is separate from its action. The action of this intelligence is the seeing and the understanding of the problem itself. The two are not separate and successive; you don't first get intelligence and then use it on the problem like a tool. It is one of the sicknesses of thinking to say that one should have the capacity first and then use it, the idea or the principle first and then apply it. This itself is the very absence of intelligence and the origin of problems. This is fragmentation. We live this way and so we speak of happiness and unhappiness, hate and love, and so on.

Questioner: Perhaps this is inherent in the structure of language.

Krishnamurti: Perhaps it is but let's not make too much fuss about it here and wander away from the issue. We are saying that intelligence, and the action of that intelligence—which is seeing the problem of unhappiness—are one indivisibly. Also that this is not separate from ending unhappiness or getting happiness.

Questioner: How am I to get that intelligence?

Krishnamurti: Have you understood what we have been saying?

Questioner: Yes.

Krishnamurti: But if you have understood you have seen that this seeing *is* intelligence. The only thing you can do is to see; you cannot cultivate intelligence in order to see. Seeing is not the cultivation of intelligence. Seeing is more important than intelligence, or happiness, or unhappiness. There is only seeing or not seeing. All the rest—happiness, unhappiness and intelligence—are just words.

Questioner: What is it, then, to see?

Krishnamurti: To see means to understand how thought creates the opposites. What thought creates is not real. To see means to understand the nature of thought, memory, conflict, ideas; to see all this as a total process is to understand. This is intelligence; seeing totally is intelligence; seeing fragmentarily is the lack of intelligence.

Questioner: I am a bit bewildered. I think I understand, but it is rather tenuous; I must go slowly. What you are saying is, see and listen completely. You say this attention is intelligence and you say that it must be immediate. One can only see *now.* I wonder if I really see now, or am I going home to think over what you have said, hoping to see later?

Krishnamurti: Then you will never see; in thinking about it you will never see it because thinking prevents seeing. Both of us have understood what it means to see. This seeing is not an essence or an abstraction or an idea. You cannot see if there is nothing to see. Now you have a problem of unhappiness. See it completely, including your wanting to be happy and how thought creates the opposite. See the search for happiness and the seeking help in order to get happiness. See disappointment, hope, fear. All of this must be seen completely, as a whole, not separately. See all this now, give your whole attention to it.

Questioner: I am still bewildered. I don't know whether I have got the essence of it, the whole point. I want to close my eyes and go into myself to see if I have really understood this thing. If I have then I have solved my problem.

LEARNING

Questioner: You have often talked about learning. I don't quite know what you mean by it. We are taught to learn at school and at the University, and life also teaches us many things—to adjust ourselves to environment and to our neighbours, to our wife or husband, to our children. We seem to learn from almost everything, but I am sure that when you speak about learning this isn't quite what you mean because you also seem to deny experience as a teacher. But when you deny experience aren't you denying all learning? After all, through experience, both in technology and in human everyday living, we learn everything we know. So could we go into this question?

Krishnamurti: Learning through experience is one thing—it is the accumulation of conditioning—and learning all the time, not only about objective things but also about oneself, is something quite different. There is the accumulation which brings about conditioning—this we know—and there is the learning which we speak about. This learning is observation—to observe without accumulation, to observe in freedom. This observation is not directed from the past. Let us keep those two things clear.

What do we learn from experience? We learn things like languages, agriculture, manners, going to the moon, medicine, mathematics. But have we learnt about war through making war? We have learnt to make war more deadly, more efficient, but we haven't learnt *not* to make war. Our experience in warfare endangers the survival of the human race. Is this learning? You may build a better house, but has experience taught you how to live more nobly inside it? We have learnt through experience that fire burns and that has become our conditioning, but we have also learnt through our conditioning that nationalism is good. Yet experience should also teach us that nationalism is deadly. All the evidence is there. The religious experience, as based on our conditioning, has separated man from man. Experience has taught us to have better food, clothes and shelter, but it has not taught us that social injustice prevents the right relationship between man and man. So experience conditions and strengthens our prejudices, our peculiar tendencies and our particular dogmas and beliefs. We do not learn what stupid nonsense all this is; we do not learn to live in the right relationship with other men. This right relationship is love. Experience teaches me to strengthen the family as a unit opposed to society and to other families. This brings about strife and division, which makes it ever more important to strengthen the family protectively, and so the vicious circle continues. We accumulate, and call this "learning through experience", but more and more this learning brings about fragmentation, narrowness and specialisation.

Questioner: Are you making out a case against technological learning and experience, against science and all accumulated knowledge? If we turn our backs on that we shall go back to savagery.

Krishnamurti: No, I am not making out such a case at all. I think we are misunderstanding each other. We said that there are two kinds of learning: accumulation through experience, and acting from that accumulation, which is the past, and which is absolutely necessary wherever the action of knowledge is necessary. We are not against this; that would be too absurd!

Questioner: Gandhi tried to keep the machine out of life and started all that business which they call "home industries" or "cottage industries" in India. Yet he used modern mechanised transport. This shows the inconsistency and hypocrisy of his position.

Krishnamurti: Let's leave other people out of this. We are saying that there are two kinds of learning—one, acting through the accumulation of knowledge and experience, and the other, learning without accumulation, but learning all the time in the very act of living. The former is absolutely necessary in all technical matters, but relationship, behaviour, are not technical matters, they are living things and you have to learn about them all the time. If you act from what you have learnt about behaviour, then it becomes mechanical and therefore relationship becomes routine.

Then there is another very important point: in all the learning which is accumulation and experience, profit is the criterion that determines the efficiency of the learning. And when the motive of profit operates in human relationships then it destroys those relationships because it brings about isolation and division. When the learning of experience and accumulation enters the domain of human behaviour, the psychological domain, then it must inevitably destroy. Enlightened self-interest on the one hand is advancement, but on the other hand it is the very seat of mischief, misery and confusion. Relationship cannot flower where there is self-interest of any kind, and that is why relationship cannot flower where it is guided by experience or memory.

Questioner: I see this, but isn't religious experience something different? I am talking about the experience gathered and passed on in religious matters—the experience of the saints and gurus, the experience of the philosophers. Isn't this kind of experience beneficial to us in our ignorance?

Krishnamurti: Not at all! The saint must be recognised by society and always conforms to society's notions of sainthood—otherwise he wouldn't be called a saint. Equally the guru must be recognised as such by his followers who are conditioned by tradition. So both the guru and the disciple are part of the cultural and religious conditioning of the particular society in which they live. When they assert that they have come into contact with reality, that they know, then you may be quite sure that what they know is not reality. What they know is their own projection from the past. So the man who says he knows, does not know. In all these so-called religious experiences a cognitive process of recognition is inherent. You can only recognise something you have known before, therefore it is of the past, therefore it is time-binding and not timeless. So-called religious experience does not bring benefit but merely conditions you according to your particular tradition, inclination, tendency and desire, and therefore encourages every form of illusion and isolation.

Questioner: Do you mean to say that you cannot experience reality?

Krishnamurti: To experience implies that there must be an experiencer, and the experiencer is the essence of all conditioning. What he experiences is the already-known.

Questioner: What do you mean when you talk about the experiencer? If there is no experiencer do you mean you disappear?

Krishnamurti: Of course. The "you" is the past and as long as the "you" remains or the "me" remains, that which is immense cannot be. The "me" with his shallow little mind, experience and knowledge, with his heart burdened with jealousies and anxieties—how can such an entity understand that which has no beginning and no ending, that which is ecstasy? So the beginning of wisdom is to understand yourself. Begin understanding yourself.

Questioner: Is the experiencer different from that which he experiences, is the challenge different from the reaction to the challenge?

Krishnamurti: The experiencer *is* the experienced, otherwise he could not recognise the experience and would not call it an experience; the experience is already in him before he recognises it. So the past is always operating and recognising itself; the new becomes swallowed up by the old. Similarly it is the reaction which determines the challenge; the challenge is the reaction, the two are not separate; without a reaction there would be no challenge. So the experience of an experiencer, or the reaction to a challenge which comes from the experiencer, are old, for they are determined by the experiencer. If you come to think of it, the word "experience" means to go through something and finish with it and not store it up, but when we talk about experience we actually mean the opposite. Every time you speak of experience you speak of something stored from which action takes place, you speak of something which you have enjoyed and demand to have again, or have disliked and fear to have repeated.

So really to live is to learn without the cumulative process.

SELF-EXPRESSION

Questioner: Expression seems to me so important. I must express myself as an artist otherwise I feel stifled and deeply frustrated. Expression is part of one's existence. As an artist it is as natural that I should give myself to it as that a man should express his love for a woman in words and gestures. But through all this expression there is a sort of pain which I don't quite understand. I think most artists would agree with me that there is deep conflict in expressing one's deepest feelings on canvas, or in any other medium. I wonder if one can ever be free of this pain, or does expression always bring pain?

Krishnamurti: What is the need of expression, and where does the suffering come into all this? Isn't one always trying to express more and more deeply, extravagantly, fully, and is one ever satisfied with what one has expressed? The deep feeling and the expression of it are not the same thing; there is a vast difference between the two, and there is always frustration when the expression doesn't correspond to the strong feeling. Probably this is one of the causes of pain, this discontent with the inadequacy of the utterance which the artist gives to his feeling. In this there is conflict and the conflict is a waste of energy. An artist has a strong feeling which is fairly authentic; he expresses it on canvas. This expression pleases some people and they buy his work; he gets money and reputation. His expression has been noticed and becomes fashionable. He refines it, pursues it, developes it, and is all the time imitating himself. This expression becomes habitual and stylised; the expression becomes more and more important and finally more important than the feeling; the feeling eventually evaporates. The artist is now left with the social consequences of being a successful painter: the market place of the salon and the gallery, the connoisseur, the critics; he is enslaved by the society for which he paints. The feeling has long since disappeared, the expression is an empty shell remaining. Consequently even this expression eventually loses its attraction because it has nothing to express; it is a gesture, a word without a meaning. This is part of the destructive process of society. This is the destruction of the good.

Questioner: Can't the feeling remain, without getting lost in expression?

Krishnamurti: When expression becomes all-important because it is pleasuable, satisfying or profitable, then there is a cleavage between expression and feeling. When the feeling *is* the expression then the conflict doesn't arise, and in this there is no contradiction and hence no conflict. But when profit and thought intervene, then this feeling is lost through greed. The passion of feeling is entiely different from the passion of expression, and most people are caught in the passion of expression. So there is always this division between the good and the pleasurable.

Questioner: Can I live without being caught in this current of greed?

Krishnamurti: If it is the feeling which is important you will never ask about expression. Either you have got the feeling or you haven't. If you ask about the expression, you are not asking about artistry but about profit. Artistry is that which is never taken into account: it is the living.

Questioner: So what is it, to live? What is it to be, and to have that feeling which is complete in itself ? I have now understood that expression is beside the point.

Krishnamurti: It is living without conflict.

PASSION

Questioner: What is passion? You've talked about it and apparently you give it a special meaning. I don't think I know that meaning. Like every man I have sexual passion and passions for superficial things like driving fast or cultivating a beautiful garden. Most of us indulge in some form of passionate activity. Talk about his special passion and you see a man's eyes sparkle. We know the word passion comes from the Greek word for suffering, but the feeling I get when you use this word is not one of suffering but rather of some driving quality like that of the wind which comes roaring out of the west, chasing the clouds and the rubbish before it. I'd like to possess that passion. How does one come by it? What is it passionate about? What *is* the passion you mean?

Krishnamurti: I think we should be clear that lust and passion are two different things. Lust is sustained by thought, driven by thought, it grows and gathers substance in thought until it explodes—sexually, or, if it is the lust for power, in its own violent forms of fulfilment. Passion is something entirely different; it is not the product of thought nor the remembrance of a past event; it is not driven by any motive of fulfilment; it is not sorrow either.

Questioner: Is all sexual passion lust? Sexual response is not always the result of thought; it may be contact as when you suddenly meet somebody whose loveliness overpowers you.

Krishnamurti: Wherever thought builds up the image of pleasure it must inevitably be lust and not the freedom of passion. If pleasure is the main drive then it is lust. When sexual feeling is born out of pleasure it is lust. If it is born out of love it is not lust, even though great delight may then be present. Here we must be clear and find out for ourselves whether love excludes pleasure and enjoyment. When you see a cloud and delight in its vastness and the light on it, there is of course pleasure, but there is a great deal more than pleasure. We are not condemning this at all. If you keep returning to the cloud in thought, or in fact, for a stimulation, then you are indulging in an imaginative flight of fancy, and obviously here pleasure and thought are the incentives operating. When you first looked at that cloud and saw its beauty there was no such incentive of pleasure operating. The beauty in sex is the absence of the "me", the ego, but the thought of sex is the affirmation of this ego, and that is pleasure. This ego is all the time either seeking pleasure or avoiding pain, wanting fulfilment and thereby inviting frustration. In all this the feeling of passion is sustained and pursued by thought, and therefore it is no longer passion but pleasure. The hope, the pursuit, of remembered passion is pleasure.

Questioner: What is passion itself, then?

Krishnamurti: It has to do with joy and ecstasy, which is not pleasure. In pleasure there is always a subtle form of effort—a seeking, striving, demanding, struggling to keep it, to get it. In passion there is no demand and therefore no struggle. In passion there is not the slightest shadow of fulfilment, therefore there can be neither frustration nor pain. Passion is the freedom from the "me", which is the centre of all fulfilment and pain. Passion does not demand because it *is,* and I am not speaking of something static. Passion is the austerity of self-abnegation in which the "you" and the "me" is not; therefore passion is the essence of life. It is this that moves and lives. But when thought brings in all the problems of having and holding, then passion ceases. Without passion creation is not possible.

Questioner: What do you mean by creation?

Krishnamurti: Freedom.

Questioner: What freedom?

Krishnamurti: Freedom from the "me" which depends on environment and is the product of environment—the me which is put together by society and thought. This freedom is clarity, the light that is not lit from the past. Passion is only the present.

Questioner: This has fired me with a strange new feeling.

Krishnamurti: That is the passion of learning.

Questioner: What particular action in my daily living will ensure that this passion is burning and operating?

Krishnamurti: Nothing will ensure it except the attention of learning, which is action, which is now. In this there is the beauty of passion, which is the total abandonment of the "me" and its time.

ORDER

Questioner: In your teaching there are a thousand details. In my living I must be able to resolve them all into one action, now, which permeates all I do, because in my living I have only the one moment right before me in which to act. What is that one action in daily living which will bring all the details of your teaching to one point, like a pyramid inverted on its point?

Krishnamurti: . . .dangerously!

Questioner: Or, to put it differently, what is the one action which will bring the total intelligence of living into focus in one instant in the present?

Krishnamurti: I think the question to ask is how to live a really intelligent, balanced, active life, in harmonious relationship with other human beings, without confusion, adjustment and misery. What is the one act that will summon this intelligence to operate in whatever you are doing? There is so much misery, poverty and sorrow in the world. What are you, as a human being, to do facing all these human problems? If you use the opportunity to help others for your own fulfilment, then it is exploitation and mischief. So we can put that aside from the beginning. The question really is, how are we to live a highly intelligent, orderly life without any kind of effort? It seems that we always approach this problem from the outside, asking ourselves, "What am I to do, confronted with all the many problems of mankind—economic, social, human?" We want to work this out in terms of the outer.

Questioner: No, I am not asking you how I can tackle or solve the problems of the world, economic, social or political. That would be too absurd! All I want to know is how to live righteously in this world exactly as it is, because it is as it is now, right here before me, and I can't will it into any other shape. I must live now in this world as it is, and in these circumstances solve all the problems of living. I am asking how to make this living a life of Dharma, which is that virtue that is not imposed from without, that does not conform to any precept, is not cultivated by any thought.

Krishnamurti: Do you mean you want to find yourself immediately, suddenly, in a state of grace which is great intelligence, innocency, love—to find yourself in this state without having a past or a future, and to act from this state?

Questioner: Yes! That is it exactly.

Krishnamurti: This has nothing to do with achievement, success or failure. There must surely be only one way to live: what is it?

Questioner: That is my question.

Krishnamurti: To have inside you that light that has no beginning and no ending, that is not lit by your desire, that is not yours or someone else's. When there is this inward light, whatever you do will always be right and true.

Questioner: How do you get that light, *now,* without all the struggle, the search, the longing, the questioning?

Krishnamurti: It is only possible when you really die to the past completely, and this can be done only when there is complete order in the brain. The brain cannot stand disorder. If there is disorder all its activities will be contradictory, confused, miserable and it will bring about mischief in itself and around itself. This order is not the design of thought, the design of obedience to a principle, to authority, or to some form of imagined goodness. It is disorder in the brain that brings about conflict; then all the various resistances cultivated by thought to escape from this disorder arise—religious and otherwise.

Questioner: How can this order be brought about to a brain that is disorderly, contradictory, in itself?

Krishnamurti: It can be done by watchfulness throughout the day, and then, before sleeping, by putting everything that has been done during the day in order. In that way the brain does not go to sleep in disorder. This does not mean that the brain hypnotises itself into a state of order when there is really disorder in and about it. There must be order during the day, and the summing up of this order before sleeping is the harmonious ending of the day. It is like a man who keeps accounts and balances them properly every evening so that he starts afresh the next day, so that when he goes to sleep his mind is quiet, empty, not worried, confused, anxious or fearful. When he wakes up there is this light which is not the product of thought or of pleasure. This light is intelligence and love. It is the negation of the disorder of the morality in which we have been brought up.

Questioner: Can I have this light immediately? That is the question I asked right at the beginning, only I put it differently.

Krishnamurti: You can have it immediately when the "me" is not. The "me" comes to an end when it sees for itself that it must end; the seeing is the light of understanding.

THE INDIVIDUAL AND THE COMMUNITY

Questioner: I don't quite know how to ask this question but I have a strong feeling that relationship between the individual and the community, these two opposing entities, has been a long history of mischief. The history of the world, of thought, of civilisation, is, after all, the history of the relationship between these two opposing entities. In all societies the individual is more or less suppressed; he must conform and fit into the pattern which the theorists have determined. The individual is always trying to break out of these patterns, and continuous battle between the two is the result. Religions talk about the individual soul as something separate from the collective soul. They emphasise the individual. In modern society—which has become so mechanical, standardised and collectively active—the individual is trying to identify himself, enquiring what he is, asserting himself. All this struggle leads nowhere. My question is, what is wrong with all this?

Krishnamurti: The only thing that really matters is that there be an action of goodness, love and intelligence in living. Is goodness individual or collective, is love personal or impersonal, is intelligence yours, mine or somebody else's? If it is yours or mine then it is not intelligence, or love, or goodness. If goodness is an affair of the individual or of the collective, according to one's particular preference or decision, then it is no longer goodness. Goodness is not in the backyard of the individual nor in the open field of the collective; goodness flowers only in freedom from both. When there is this goodness, love and intelligence, then action is not in terms of the individual or the collective. Lacking goodness, we divide the world into the individual and the collective, and further divide the collective into innumerable groups according to religion, nationality and class. Having created these divisions we try to bridge them by forming new groups which are again divided from other groups. We see that every great religion supposedly exists to bring about the brotherhood of man and, in actual fact, prevents it. We always try to reform that which is already corrupt. We don't eradicate corruption fundamentally but simply rearrange it.

Questioner: Are you saying that we need not waste time in these endless bargainings between the individual and the collective, or try to prove that they are different or that they are similar? Are you saying that only goodness, love and intelligence are the issue, and that these lie beyond the individual or the collective?

Krishnamurti: Yes.

Questioner: So the real question seems to be how love, goodness and intelligence can act in daily living.

Krishnamurti: If these act, then the question of the individual and the collective is academic.

Questioner: How are they to act?

Krishnamurti: They can act only in relationship: all existence is in relationship. So the first thing is to become aware of one's relationship to everything and everybody, and to see how in this relationship the "me" is born and acts. This "me" is the action of the human heart and mind; it is the "me" that is both the collective and the individual; it is the "me" that separates; it is the "me" that acts collectively or individually, the "me" that creates heaven and hell. To be aware of this is to understand it. And the understanding of it is the ending of it. The ending of it is goodness, love and intelligence.

MEDITATION AND ENERGY

Questioner: This morning I should like to go into the deeper meaning, or deeper sense, of meditation. I have practised many forms of it, including a little Zen. There are various schools which teach awareness but they all seem rather superficial, so can we leave all that aside and go into it more deeply?

Krishnamurti: We must also set aside the whole meaning of authority, because in meditation any form of authority, either one's own or the authority of another, becomes an impediment and prevents freedom—prevents a freshness, a newness. So authority, conformity and imitation must be set aside completely. Otherwise you merely imitate, follow what has been said, and that makes the mind very dull and stupid. In that there is no freedom. Your past experience may guide, direct or establish a new path, and so even that must go. Then only can one go into this very deep and extraordinarily important thing called meditation. Meditation is the essence of energy.

Questioner: For many years I have tried to see that I do not become a slave to the authority of someone else or to a pattern. Of course there is a danger of deceiving myself but as we go along I shall probably find out. But when you say that meditation is the essence of energy, what do you mean by the words energy and meditation?

Krishnamurti: Every movement of thought, every action demands energy. Whatever you do or think needs energy, and this energy can be dissipated through conflict, through various forms of unnecessary thought, emotional pursuits and senti-mental activities. Energy is wasted in conflict which arises in duality, in the "me" and the "not-me", in the division between the observer and the observed, the thinker and the thought. When this wastage is no longer taking place there is a quality of energy which can be called an awareness—an awareness in which there is no evaluation, judgement, condemnation or comparison but merely an attentive observation, a seeing of things exactly as they are, both inwardly and outwardly, without the interference of thought, which is the past.

Questioner: This I find very difficult to understand. If there were no thought at all, would it be possible to recognise a tree, or my wife or neighbour? Recognition is necessary, isn't it, when you look at a tree or the woman next door?

Krishnamurti: When you observe a tree is recognition neces-sary? When you look at that tree, do you say it is a tree or do you just look? If you begin to recognise it as an elm, an oak or a mango tree then the past interferes with direct observation. In the same way, when you look at your wife, if you look with memories of annoyances or pleasures you are not really looking at her but at the image which you have in your mind about her. That prevents direct perception: direct perception does not need recognition. Outward recognition of your wife, your chil-dren, your house or your neighbour may be necessary, but why should there be an interference of the past in the eyes, the mind and the heart? Doesn't it prevent you from seeing clearly? When you condemn or have an opinion about something, that opinion or prejudice distorts observation.

Questioner: Yes, I see that. That subtle form of recognition does distort, I see that. You say all these interferences of thought are a waste of energy. You say observe without any form of recogni-tion, condemnation, judgement; observe without naming, for that naming, recognition, condemnation is a waste of energy. That can be logically and actually understood. Then there is the next point which is the division, the separateness, or, rather, as you have often put it in your talks, the space that exists between the observer and the observed which creates duality; you say that this also is a waste of energy and brings about conflict. I find everything you say logical but I find it extraordinarily difficult to remove that space, to bring about harmony between the observer and the observed. How is this to be done?

Krishnamurti: There is no how. The how means a system, a method, a practice which becomes mechanical. Again we have to be rid of the significance of the word "how".

Questioner: Is it possible? I know the word possible implies a future, an effort, a striving to bring about harmony, but one must use certain words. I hope we can go beyond those words, so is it possible to bring about a union between the observer and the observed?

Krishnamurti: The observer is always casting its shadow on the thing it observes. So one must understand the structure and the nature of the observer, not how to bring about a union between the two. One must understand the movement of the observer and in that understanding perhaps the observer comes to an end. We must examine what the observer is: it is the past with all its memories, conscious and unconscious, its racial inheritance, its accumulated experience which is called knowledge, its reactions. The observer is really the conditioned entity. He is the one who asserts that *he is,* that *I am.* In protecting himself, he resists, dominates, seeking comfort and security. The observer then sets himself apart as something different from that which he observes, inwardly or outwardly. This brings about a duality and from this duality there is conflict, which is the wastage of energy. To be aware of the observer, his movement, his self-centred activity, his assertions, his prejudices, one must be aware of all these unconscious movements which build the separatist feeling that he is different. It must be observed without any form of evaluation, without like and dislike; just observe it in daily life, in its relationships. When this observation is clear, isn't there then a freedom from the observer?

Questioner: You are saying, Sir, that the observer is really the ego; you are saying that as long as the ego exists, he must resist, divide, separate, for in this separation, this division, he feels alive. It gives him vitality to resist, to fight, and he has become accustomed to that battle; it is his way of living. Are you not saying that this ego, this "I", must dissolve through an observation in which there is no sense of like or dislike, no opinion or judgement, but only the observing of this "I" in action? But can such a thing really take place? Can I look at myself so completely, so truly, without distortion? You say that when I do look at myself so clearly then the "I" has no movement at all. And you say this is part of meditation?

Krishnamurti: Of course. This *is* meditation.

Questioner: This observation surely demands extraordinary self-discipline.

Krishnamurti: What do you mean by self-discipline? Do you mean disciplining the self by putting him in a strait-jacket, or do you mean learning about the self, the self that asserts, that dominates, that is ambitious, violent and so on—learning about it? The learning is, in itself, discipline. The word discipline means to learn and when there is learning, not accumulating, when there is actual learning, which needs attention, that learning brings about its own responsibility, its own activity, its own dimensions: so there is no discipline as something imposed upon it. Where there is learning there is no imitation, no conformity, no authority. If this is what you mean by the word discipline, then surely there is freedom to learn?

Questioner: You are taking me too far and perhaps too deeply, and I can't quite go with you where this learning is concerned. I see very clearly that the self as the observer must come to an end. It is logically so, and there must be no conflict: that is very clear. But you are saying that this very observation is learning and in learning there is always accumulation; this accumulation becomes the past. Learning is an additive process, but you are apparently giving it a different meaning altogether. From what I have understood you are saying that learning is a constant movement without accumulation. Is that so? Can learning be without accumulation?

Krishnamurti: Learning is its own action. What generally happens is that having learnt—we act upon what we have learnt. So there is division between the past and action, and hence there is a conflict between what should be and what is, or what has been and what is. We are saying that there can be action in the very movement of learning: that is, learning is doing; it is not a question of having learnt and then acting. This is very important to understand because having learnt, and acting from that accumulation, is the very nature of the "me", the "I", the ego or whatever name one likes to give it. The "I" is the very essence of the past and the past impinges on the present and so on into the future. In this there is constant division. Where there is a learning there is a constant movement; there is no accumulation which can become the "I".

Questioner: But in the technological field there must be accumulated knowledge. One can't fly the Atlantic or run a car, or even do most of the ordinary daily things without knowledge.

Krishnamurti: Of course not, Sir; such knowledge is absolutely necessary. But we are talking about the psychological field in which the "I" operates. The "I" can use technological knowledge in order to achieve something, a position or prestige; the "I" can use that knowledge to function, but if in functioning the "I" interferes, things begin to go wrong, for the "I", through technical means, seeks status. So the "I" is not concerned merely with knowledge in scientific fields; it is using it to achieve something else. It is like a musician who uses the piano to become famous. What he is concerned with is fame and not the beauty of the music in itself or for itself. We are not saying that we must get rid of technological knowledge; on the contrary, the more technological knowledge there is the better living conditions will be. But the moment the "I" uses it, things begin to go wrong.

Questioner: I think I begin to understand what you are saying. You are giving quite a different meaning and dimension to the word learning, which is marvellous. I am beginning to grasp it. You are saying that meditation is a movement of learning and in that there is freedom to learn about everything, not only about meditation, but about the way one lives, drives, eats, talks, everything.

Krishnamurti: As we said, the essence of energy is meditation. To put it differently—so long as there is a meditator there is no meditation. If he attempts to achieve a state described by others, or some flash of experience. . . .

Questioner: If I may interrupt you, Sir, are you saying that learning must be constant, a flow, a line without any break, so that learning and action are one, or a constant movement? I don't know what word to use, but I am sure you understand what I mean. The moment there is a break between learning, action and meditation, that break is a disharmony, that break is conflict. In that break there is the observer and the observed and hence the whole wastage of energy; is that what you are saying?

Krishnamurti: Yes, that is what we mean. Meditation is not a state; it is a movement, as action is a movement. And as we said just now, when we separate action from learning, then the observer comes between the learning and the action; then he becomes important; then he uses action and learning for ulterior motives. When this is very clearly understood as one harmonious movement of acting, of learning, of meditation, there is no wastage of energy and this is the beauty of meditation. There is only one movement. Learning is far more important than meditation or action. To learn there must be complete freedom, not only consciously but deeply, inwardly—a total freedom. And in freedom there is this movement of learning, acting, meditating as a harmonious whole. The word whole not only means health but holy. So learning is holy, acting is holy, meditation is holy. This is really a sacred thing and the beauty is in itself and not beyond it.

ENDING THOUGHT

Questioner: I wonder what you really mean by ending thought. I talked to a friend about it and he said it is some kind of oriental nonsense. To him thought is the highest form of intelligence and action, the very salt of life, indispensable. It has created civilisation, and all relationship is based on it. All of us accept this, from the greatest thinker to the humblest labourer. When we don't think we sleep, vegetate or day-dream; we are vacant, dull and unproductive, whereas when we are awake we are thinking, doing, living, quarrelling: these are the only two states we know. You say, be beyond both—beyond thought and vacant inactivity. What do you mean by this?

Krishnamurti: Very simply put, thought is the response of memory, the past. The past is an infinity or a second ago. When thought acts it is this past which is acting as memory, as experience, as knowledge, as opportunity. All will is desire based on this past and directed towards pleasure or the avoidance of pain. When thought is functioning it is the past, therefore there is no new living at all; it is the past living in the present, modifying itself and the present. So there is nothing new in life that way, and when something new is to be found there must be the absence of the past, the mind must not be cluttered up with thought, fear, pleasure and everything else. Only when the mind is uncluttered can the new come into being, and for this reason we say that thought must be still, operating only when it has to —objectively, efficiently. All continuity is thought; when there is continuity there is nothing new. Do you see how important this is? It's really a question of life itself. Either you live in the past, or you live totally differently: that is the whole point.

Questioner: I think I do see what you mean, but how in the world is one to end this thought? When I listen to the blackbird there is thought telling me instantly it is the blackbird; when I walk down the street thought tells me I am walking down the street and tells me all I recognise and see; when I play with the notion of not thinking it is again thought that plays this game. All meaning and understanding and communication are thought. Even when I am not communicating with someone else I am doing so with myself. When I am awake, I think, when I am asleep, I think. The whole structure of my being is thought. Its roots lie far deeper than I know. All I think and do and all I am is thought, thought creating pleasure and pain, appetites, longings, resolutions, conclusions, hopes, fears and questions. Thought commits murder and thought forgives. So how can one go beyond it? Isn't it thought again which seeks to go beyond it?

Krishnamurti: We both said, when thought is still, something new can be. We both saw that point clearly and to understand it clearly is the ending of thought.

Questioner: But that understanding is also thought.

Krishnamurti: Is it? You assume that it is thought, but is it, actually?

Questioner: It is a mental movement with meaning, a communication to oneself.

Krishnamurti: If it is a communication to oneself it is thought. But is understanding a mental movement with meaning?

Questioner: Yes it is.

Krishnamurti: The meaning of the word and the understanding of that meaning is thought. That is necessary in life. There thought must function efficiently. It is a technological matter.

But you are not asking that. You are asking how thought, which is the very movement of life as you know it, can come to an end. Can it only end when you die? That is really your question, isn't it?

Questioner: Yes.

Krishnamurti: That is the right question. Die! Die to the past, to tradition.

Questioner: But how?

Krishnamurti: The brain is the source of thought. The brain is matter and thought is matter. Can the brain—with all its reactions and its immediate responses to every challenge and demand—can that brain be very still? It is not a question of ending thought, but of whether the brain can be completely still. Can it act with full capacity when necessary and otherwise be still? This stillness is not physical death.

See what happens when the brain is completely still.

See what happens.

Questioner: In that space there was the blackbird, the green tree, the blue sky, the man hammering next door, the sound of the wind in the trees and my own heartbeat, the total quietness of the body. That is all.

Krishnamurti: If there was recognition of the blackbird singing, then the brain was active, was interpreting. It was not still. This really demands tremendous alertness and discipline, the watching that brings its own discipline, not imposed or brought about by your unconscious desire to achieve a result or a pleasurable new experience. Therefore during the day thought must operate effectively, sanely, and also watch itself.

Questioner: That is easy, but what about going beyond it?

Krishnamurti: Who is asking this question? Is it the desire to experience something new or is it the enquiry? If it is the enquiry, then you must enquire and investigate the whole business of thinking and be completely familiar with it, know all its tricks and subtleties. If you have done this you will know that the question of going beyond thought is an empty one. Going beyond thought is knowing what thought is.

THE NEW HUMAN BEING

Questioner: I am a reformer, a social worker. Seeing the extraordinary injustice there is in the world, my whole life has been dedicated to reform. I used to be a Communist but I can't go along with Communism any more, it has ended in tyrany. Nevertheless, I am still dedicated to reforming society so that man can live in dignity, beauty and freedom, and realise the potential which nature seems to have given him, and which he himself seems always to have stolen from his fellow man. In America there is a certain kind of freedom, and yet standardisation and propaganda are very strong there—all the mass media exert a tremendous pressure on the mind. It seems that the power of television, this mechanical thing that man has invented, has developed its own personality, its own will, its own momentum; and though probably nobody—perhaps not even any one group —is deliberately using it to influence society, its trend shapes the very souls of our children. And this is the same in varying degrees in all democracies. In China there seems to be no hope at all for the dignity or freedom of man, while in India the government is weak, corrupt and inefficient. It seems to me that all the social injustice in the world absolutely must be changed. I want passionately to do something about it, yet I don't know where to begin to tackle it.

Krishnamurti: Reform needs further reform, and this is an endless process. So let us look at it differently. Let us put aside the whole thought of reform; let us wipe it out of our blood. Let us completely forget this idea of wanting to reform the world.

Then let us see actually what is happening, right throughout the world. Political parties always have a limited programme which, even if fulfilled, invariably brings about mischief, which then has to be corrected once again. We are always talking about political action as being a most important action, but political action is not the way. Let us put it out of our minds. All social and economic reforms come under this category. Then there is the religious formula of action based on belief, idealism, dogmatism, conformity to some so-called divine recipe. In this is involved authority and acceptance, obedience and the utter denial of freedom. Though religions talk of peace on earth they contribute to the disorder because they are a factor of division. Also the churches have always taken some political stand in times of crisis, so they are really political bodies, and we have seen that all political action is divisive. The churches have never really denied war: on the contrary they have waged war. So when one puts aside the religious recipes, as one puts aside the political formulas—what is left, and what is one to do? Naturally civic order must be maintained: you have to have water in the taps. If you destroy civic order you have to start again from the beginning. So, what is one to do?

Questioner: That is what I am actually asking you.

Krishnamurti: Be concerned with radical change, with total revolution. The only revolution is the revolution between man and man, between human beings. That is our only concern. In this revolution there are no blueprints, no ideologies, no conceptual utopias. We must take the fact of the actual relationship between men and change that radically. That is the real thing. And this revolution must be immediate, it must not take time. It is not achieved through evolution, which is time.

Questioner: What do you mean? All historical changes have taken place in time; none of them has been immediate. You are proposing something quite inconceivable.

Krishnamurti: If you take time to change, do you suppose that life is in suspension during the time it takes to change? It isn't in suspension. Everything you are trying to change is being modified and perpetuated by the environment, by life itself. So there is no end to it. It is like trying to clean the water in a tank which is constantly being refilled with dirty water. So time is out.

Now, what is to bring about this change? It cannot be will, or determination, or choice, or desire, because all these are part of the entity that has to be changed. So we must ask what actually is possible, without the action of will and assertiveness which is always the action of conflict.

Questioner: Is there any action which is not the action of will and assertiveness?

Krishnamurti: Instead of asking this question let us go much deeper. Let us see that actually it is *only* the action of will and assertiveness that needs to be changed at all, because the only mischief in relationship is conflict, between individuals or within individuals, and conflict *is* will and assertiveness. Living without such action does not mean that we live like vegetables. Conflict is our main concern. All the social maladies you mentioned are the projection of this conflict in the heart of each human being. The only possible change is a radical transformation of yourself in all your relationships, not in some vague future, but now.

Questioner: But how can I completely eradicate this conflict in myself, this contradiction, this resistance, this conditioning? I understand what you mean intellectually, but I can only change when I feel it passionately, and I don't feel it passionately. It is merely an idea to me; I don't see it with my heart. If I try to act on this intellectual understanding I am in conflict with another, deeper, part of myself.

Krishnamurti: If you really see this contradiction passionately, then that very perception is the revolution. If you see in yourself this division between the mind and the heart, actually see it, not conceive of it theoretically, but see it, then the problem comes to an end. A man who is passionate about the world and the necessity for change, must be free from political activity, religious conformity and tradition—which means, free from the weight of time, free from the burden of the past, free from all the action of will: this is the new human being. This only is the social, psychological and even the political revolution.